From Porn
To the Pulpit...

Minister

Danielle Williams

From Porn to the Pulpit
The Danielle Williams Story Copyright © 2011 by Danielle Williams V.2

ISBN-13: 978-1477673829
ISBN-10: 1477673822

All rights reserved. No part of this book may be reproduced or transmitted in any form or by any means, electronic or mechanical, including photocopying, recording, or by any information storage and retrieval system, without permission in writing from the copyright owner.
SOV Books Norwalk, California www.saintsofvalue.org. A division of Vienna Schilling Books
Fair Oaks, California www.viennaschilling.us

Printed in the United States of America

Meet the Author

Minister Danielle Williams

Acknowledgments

First, I give all honor to CHRIST JESUS who is the head of my life, my entire life, and my everything. Without Him I would not be here. I thank Him for never giving up on me even when I gave up on myself. He is my inspiration, my hero, and the reason I smile. I will forever be dedicated to Him. Thank You for being in the fire with me.

To my mother, Vanessa Williams: I love you very much. The Lord made you my mother and me your daughter; and because of that I will love and honor you all the days of my life. I believe our latter days will be better than our former!

I would also like to thank my grandparents, Tommy and Gloria Garner, also known as my angels. Thank you for praying me through. It worked; and I love you very much for that.

To my cousin, Betty Riggs; thank you for encouraging me to write this book; and a special thanks to Pastor Justin Cox. God used you to get me to where I am today. Thank you for taking a risk on my story, and putting it out there for the world to see.

I would like to send a special thanks to Minister Paulette Green and Pastor Jarvis Hines. You both are more than Pastors to me; you are my family. I praise God for the both of you. Mrs. Vanessa Hines, I love you sis!

I also want to thank my real friends for putting up with my mess, my trials, and my triumphs: Pierra 'Princess' LaMarr, Kiaira 'Koko' Stephens, Rozell 'Wowie' Anderson, and Tearea 'Mercedes' Colton. You have been by my side throughout my transition and I am so thankful for you. (If I left anyone's name out, don't hold it against me; you know I love you too!)

I want to thank all the people who doubted me and said I would never make anything of myself. If you hadn't said those things I wouldn't have worked so hard to get to where I am today.

Last, but not least, I want to thank all of you readers not only because you purchased this book, but because I want to thank you for trusting what God has done in my life and what He can do in yours as well. I pray that my story will be a blessing to you. Feel free to write me at expornstar3@yahoo.com. I look forward to hearing from you. God Bless you all.

The names in this book have been changed.

Table of Contents

Introduction..................	i
Chapter 1 My Daddy...........................	1
Chapter 2 Mom, Here I Come!.............	19
Chapter 3 I'm Gay...And I Don't Mean 'Happy'!....	41
Chapter 4 Looking For Love.........................	49
Chapter 5 The Beginning of Disaster.......................	63
Chapter 6 Pimps and Prostitutes............................	77
Chapter 7 Xstacy...	111
Chapter 8 The Addiction..............................	119
Chapter 9 Porn..	125
Chapter 10 Please Don't Kill Me............................	151
Chapter 11 New York....................................	167
Chapter 12 God Help Me!.............................	189
Chapter 13 The Breakdown.........................	205
Chapter 14 A New Beginning.....................	217
Chapter 15 There is Hope!.........................	223

Pornography Statistics

Introduction

If you purchased this book then you already know that I was in the porn industry. One of the reasons I wrote this book was to show people why I made some of the bad choices you will read about. Whenever I appear at speaking engagements, I always inform the audience that there is always a reason as to why people make certain decisions.

No one just wakes up and says, "I want to be a prostitute!" Children do not grow up with hopes of becoming a stripper or porn star. There are things that take place in people's lives that cause them to react in certain ways.

If you know someone who is acting out or behaving in an inappropriate way, I promise that after you read this book you will take a different approach in how you deal with them. The best advice I can give you when reaching out to someone who is misbehaving, is instead of yelling and screaming at them, or disowning them, sit down and find out what is causing the problem.

Often times when people are behaving a certain way they are crying out for help but just don't know how to simply ask. Many children have been raped, beaten or molested and decided to keep silent out of fear. So they start to rebel or act out because of the pain and hurt they are experiencing. Most women start a promiscuous lifestyle because they have experienced abuse in one way or another.

In writing this book, my aim was to bring hope to those who have chosen a fallen path, and to bring light to what goes on in the dark world of prostitution and porn.

Another reason why I wrote this book was to let every human being know that God is still in the saving business! He is still able to heal, deliver and set people free. I never would have imagined that I would be where I am today…but God.

I wasn't worthy to be chosen, but He saw something in me that no one else did. 1st Corinthians 1:27 declares, "But God has chosen the foolish things of the world to confound the wise; and God has chosen the weak things of the world to confound the things which are mighty." It's very important for church people not to judge someone, even when they are not living right. God is the Alpha and the Omega, the Beginning and the End. He is the only one who knows someone's future; not you. So be very careful about who you point your finger at. Instead of being judgmental, pray for that individual and believe that God can and will deliver them. He did it for me and the same God that saved me can save everyone else!

Chapter 1

My Daddy

On February 25, 1989, I was born to my mother, Vanessa, and my father, Dee, in Los Angeles, California. They were married, but not happily. My parents fought like cats and dogs, mainly because of my father's infidelity and my mother's mismanagement of money.

My mother, who was born and raised in Compton, had a very hardcore exterior. Although very kind and fun to be around, you did not want to get on her bad side. My father was of Jamaican decent and had a very bad alcohol problem, so they often collided.

My house was dysfunctional and many times I

From Porn to the Pulpit

witnessed them beat each other to bloody pulps. Although my mother is a woman, that never stopped her from picking up an object and busting my dad in his head with it. As they fought each other, I always got caught in the crossfire, as they fell on top of me. One time, my dad busted my mother's car windows. The glass broke and sprayed all over me as I sat in the backseat.

Other times, shots would be fired while I was in the house. My mother also stabbed my dad in the neck with a butcher's knife as I sat watching only a few feet away. One thing they had in common was that they both loved to drink. That might have been the only thing they ever had in common. I do believe they loved each other at one point, but in the end they divorced.

When the time came they decided that I should stay in Carson with my daddy. Although he had a few issues, alcohol being one of them, he treated me like a queen. I was Daddy's little girl. He became my mother and father, teaching me how to wash and iron clothes, how to cook and clean, and how to become a young lady.

Daddy involved me in a lot of activities, such as tap dancing and piano lessons. I also ran track and

Daddy

danced on the drill team as Daddy cheered from the sideline. They say the first man a girl falls in love with is her father, and if that statement were true, then I was head over heels! Our relationship was like no other. We were inseparable; when you saw Daddy, you saw me too. The fact that our birthdays are on the same day, made us even closer.

Anything I wanted, he gave to me; anywhere I wanted to go, he took me there. He pampered me. Even with the absence of my mother, I felt so loved. I believed he went above and beyond as a father. Although he'd never admit it, I believe Daddy had outside children as well, but his only focus was on me. He was an excellent father, but Daddy was a ladies' man. He had multiple women of all ethnicities. I would find myself getting jealous of the time he spent with them, but he always assured me that I was his Queen. I don't understand why they liked him because he was extremely abusive towards them. I used to watch in awe as he broke their noses, dragged them through the house, and put their heads in the toilet. He constantly bad mouthed them and locked them up in the garage

From Porn to the Pulpit

from time to time, and did it all right in front of me. He even demanded that they abort their pregnancies by him. He treated them horribly, and yet they never left him. It seemed like the more he hurt them, the more they wanted to stay with him.

Being young and having no understanding of the world, I thought it was normal for a man to treat a woman like that, since this was the only thing being shown to me. I felt if Daddy was doing it, then it had to be okay.

Daddy would drop me off at a babysitter's house because of the time he spent at work, and with his women. The sitter was a very nice lady, but whenever she ran her errands, she left the younger kids in the care of her teenage son. I was eight years old at the time and her son was around fourteen, and for some reason, out of all the other little girls there, I was his pick. Whenever his mother left, he would make me come into his bedroom, lie on his bed and unbutton my pants. He started off by

Daddy

kissing me and putting his hands in my underwear. Eventually, he inserted his fingers inside of me. When he had enough of that, he stuck toys in me which was very painful. The whole time he was doing this, he had a smile on his face, as he was being turned on more and more by my eight-year old body.

When I told him to stop, he hit me and told me to shut up. I don't know how I felt emotionally at the time other than I knew he wasn't supposed to be doing that. I just wanted him to stop. He always told me that he would cut my throat if I ever said anything about it, and out of fear I never told my dad or anyone.

The abuse continued for a couple of months, sometimes while his mother was in the other room. She had no clue that I was being molested by her son. Being tired of his punches to my face and arms, and the pain in my vagina from his fingers and toys, I tried to convince my dad that I was too old for a babysitter and that I was able to take care of myself. He actually agreed and the babysitter nightmare finally came to an end.

My father and I were very close, but we didn't see eye to eye about one particular thing. I was around the age of ten and I wanted to look more like a young lady, but Daddy wasn't feeling that. My hair and nails were always done, but he dressed me like a boy. Anything opposite of that was unacceptable.

I was tired of being teased by the other girls about my "tomboy" looks. They called me Daniel instead of Danielle because I played basketball with the neighborhood boys, instead of playing with Barbie's I rode dirt bikes. Nothing about me was feminine. In other words, I was my dad's 'son.' He did anything and everything he could to make sure that I didn't get any attention from boys.

Under my dad's care I became a straight-A student, spelling bee champion, honor-roll student, and top of my class. He had high hopes of me

Daddy

graduating from college and becoming a lawyer. My dad was very involved with my schooling and wanted to know everything that was going on.

In November of 1999, I had a parent-teacher meeting and, of course, my dad attended. My teacher mentioned how smart I was, and how I was the best student in her class, but then she told my dad about an incident that happened during lunch the other day. She saw me kiss a boy and had called me in to talk to me about it. Immediately, my dad went from being a proud parent to having a look of disgust on his face. It was odd to me that, after all the great things my teacher said about me, all he heard was that I kissed a boy. It enraged him to an inexplicable point. I knew my dad could get angry (mainly when he was drunk), but I had never seen him like this. The ride home was very intense and frightening. Don't get me wrong; Daddy was definitely a disciplinarian when necessary, but this time it was different. He was so furious that he ran stop lights to get me home and whoop me. I knew that I was going to get into trouble because Daddy didn't want me to interact with boys, but I couldn't understand why it made him this angry. In the car he yelled and cursed at me. Then he slapped me so hard in the mouth that he knocked my tooth out. My dad raised me not to cry, so I didn't let one tear drop. It seemed like we got from the school to the house in twenty seconds. When we entered the house, I knew it would go from bad to worse. My dad shut all the doors and windows, told me to go to my room and take my clothes off. I didn't hesitate, but I was not prepared for what was about to happen next.

He walked into my room with rage in his eyes. I was horrified because I had never seen him like this before. I stood there naked as he started the assault. The first blow was to my back with a wooden paddle. The next object was a belt, and I do mean the buckle. The second round consisted of the paddle and belt together followed by blows from his fist; mainly to my face and the front and back of my naked body.

Daddy

One would think that the intensity of my screams would cause him to stop, but it didn't. He paused for just a moment because the phone rang. Then he told me to go and do my homework. I thought my misery was over, but it was just getting started.

I put my clothes back on and sat at the kitchen table with my books. He never explained why I had to strip naked in order to take this beating. He very well could have done so with my clothes on.

As I sat there at the kitchen table, bleeding and in pain, he sat only a few feet away on the living room couch, still screaming at me for kissing the boy at school. This seemed to rekindle his madness and he came after me again with full force. This time, he lifted me up from the chair by my throat to the ceiling, and then slammed me to the floor like a sack of potatoes. Then, the blows came again from his fist. For a ten-year-old girl to be beaten by a big, muscular, thirty-three-year-old man, felt like getting smashed by bricks.

I took this beating for hours until my body couldn't take it anymore. I passed out not once, but twice. One would think that my loving father would help me up, but nope! He stood over me to see if I was still breathing, and when I finally opened my eyes, he sat back on the couch and told me to get in the bathtub.

The warm water from the tub burned the welts on my skin. The pain was so excruciating I wanted to scream, but I couldn't. Just when I thought it was over, he assaulted me again. My dad busted through the bathroom door shouting, "You wanna kiss boys? I'm not raising you to be a hoe!"

Then, he grabbed my face, pried open my mouth, and tried to physically rip my tongue out, knocking out another tooth. He pushed me under the bath water and all I could do was look up at my Daddy in disbelief. I couldn't believe that the man I loved more than myself was trying to drown me. I thank God that he came back to his senses and let me up before it was too late.

The next morning came quickly, or maybe it just seemed like that, because I was getting beaten all night long. When I woke up for school I stood in the mirror and looked at my distorted face. It was hard for me to believe that my daddy could do this to me.

I don't believe that he saw how bad my face looked that morning, because if he had, he would never have let me out of the house. When I arrived

Daddy

at school the teacher took one look at me and dropped to the floor in tears. All she kept saying was "Oh my God, I'm so sorry! I'm so sorry!"

She took me to the school office, filed a child abuse report against my father, and the police showed up. They took me to a nearby hospital and my mother was called. When Mom got there, I remember her saying to the doctor, "That's not my daughter!" I was so disfigured that my own mother didn't recognize me. Once the doctors convinced her that it was really me, she ran over to me in tears and wrapped me in her arms.

After that my dad went to jail and was then transferred to a mental facility. Later I found out that he had a mental disorder. He was Bipolar and slightly Schizophrenic, which caused the psychotic episode.

Under court order, I was removed from his home and sent to live with my grandmother, "Ericka." She was my dad's mother and I didn't like her very much. She had a huge house in Orange County, a nice car, and plenty of money, but there was one thing that she didn't have…white skin.

Ericka's parents were Jamaican but she was raised in Louisiana, and for some crazy reason she didn't like it, nor did she acknowledge her background. She never said it, but she desperately wanted to be Caucasian. I've never seen so much self-hatred in all my life. She tried to change me too. She put me in a predominantly white, private school and I was actually the only black girl in the entire school. She wanted me to talk differently and act differently, but I had a hard time doing that. I didn't see anything wrong with being a black girl from Los Angeles.

A year went by and my dad was able to contact me. I was so happy when I heard his voice, that my heart skipped a beat. Ericka asked me if I wanted to go back and live with him, and immediately I said yes!

Despite what my dad did to me, I loved and missed him with all my heart. He was everything to me. Against court orders, we arranged for him to pick me up from school the following day. The anticipation nearly killed me. When the bell rang I was the first one out of class. I hadn't seen him for a year, so I wasn't sure what to look for, but when he called my name the wait and worry was finally over. I turned around and ran to him at full speed and squeezed him as tight as I could. That day I

Daddy

was made whole again.

I moved back with my dad and had just turned twelve. A whole year had passed and things were going well with Daddy and I. He never put his hands on me ever again and I never gave him a reason to.

In the summer of 2001, my dad mentioned to me that he wanted to go to Las Vegas to visit his father, my Papa. I was so excited and couldn't wait to see my grandfather.

Papa was loud and 'ghetto' and he loved to get drunk, but he was so much fun to be around. He had other grandchildren, but I was his favorite and he made sure I knew it. Papa spoiled me rotten. He gave me everything I wanted. He and Daddy had a weird relationship; one minute they were best friends, and the next they were at each other's throats. Daddy blamed Papa for not being in his life when he was younger, but Ericka wouldn't let him during those years. Papa tried to explain that to him over and over, but Daddy could never accept that.

We weren't at Papa's house long before they started arguing. My dad told me that he was leaving and going to a casino to blow off some steam. He said he would be right back, so I walked him to the car and gave him a hug and kiss, not knowing that this would be the last time.

Daddy drove off and didn't call or come back to Papa's house that night. A few days went by and although I worried, I didn't cry. Daddy would always say, "Why cry? Tears can't change the situation."

Later on that night, I heard Papa screaming at the top of his lungs, so I ran downstairs. He was on the phone saying, "You're a sorry excuse for a man! How could you leave your daughter like that?"

I went to him and asked what was going on. He said that I was going to stay with him for now. My heart dropped. I ran upstairs and ignored everything my dad ever said about crying. I collapsed to the floor and screamed 'till I lost my voice. I cried so hard, it felt like he died and this was his funeral. That's exactly what happened that night, because he was, in fact, dead to me. I couldn't understand why he would want to break my heart. What did I do to him? The sadness and hurt I felt quickly turned to anger. How dare he do this to me again!

Time passed and I got used to my new life in

Daddy

Vegas with Papa, but I didn't get along with his girlfriend, "Leah." For some unknown reason, that woman did not like me. I always thought that maybe she was jealous of the relationship that Papa and I had. He spent most of his time with me, taking the attention away from her. He gave me any and everything I needed and wanted, which put a dent in her needs and wants.

She would always find reasons to put me on punishment, or pick with me about something. I thought it was interesting that I couldn't get along with the women in my life, but the men loved me.

My mother wasn't there, but my father was. I didn't get along with my grandmother, Ericka, but Papa and I had a great relationship. Then, Leah didn't like me for whatever reason. I couldn't understand what it was about me that they didn't like. I wasn't a bad kid (yet), but I never allowed it to bother me because Papa worked hard to make me feel loved, since my mother and father were now out of my life.

Things got even better when he and his two stepdaughters changed me out of my boyish ways. I began dressing like a girl, which got me some major attention from boys; one in particular named

From Porn to the Pulpit

"Mike," whom I had my eye on since arriving in Vegas.

Although he was eighteen and I was only twelve, that didn't stop us from talking. I knew at an early age that I was attracted to older boys. Every girl that I was around was sexually active and I was the only virgin, never fitting into any conversations about what guy they had sex with, or who was sleeping with whom. The peer pressure started to get to me, and since Mike and I were dating for a few months I decided to give him my virginity.

I had it all planned out. It was a Friday night and Papa was asleep; not even a fire could wake him. I snuck Mike upstairs into my bedroom and I was both excited and nervous about what was going to happen. I felt a little embarrassed wearing the lingerie that I stole from Wal-Mart earlier that day, but when he saw me he told me I looked pretty. Never hearing that from a boy before, made me want to sleep with him even more.

The experience was painful and uncomfortable at first, but in the end, I felt amazing because of what he did to me, emotionally. Mike and I stayed together even though we had sex only once. I didn't want to go through that painful process again and

Daddy

he was okay with that. That's why I liked him so much. He never pressured me into doing anything I didn't want to do.

For the moment I forgot how angry I was at my dad, because I was so happy when I was with Mike. He filled the void that my dad left in my heart. Unfortunately, it all ended when he moved back to Belize with his family. My happy days were over.

Suddenly, my anger got the best of me, and it was more so directed towards boys. The sight of them turned me into a monster. When I looked at boys, I saw the babysitter's son molesting me. I saw my dad beating me. I saw Mike leaving me, and I just became so furious.

The time came for me to be enrolled in school, and while there, I fought with boys regularly which got me suspended often; but one day in particular, I lost it. There was a boy in my class who made fun of me for not having a father, and that was it. I never let anyone get away with that. I beat him up with a math book, until school security came and pulled me off of him. Although my dad was not there I didn't allow anyone to speak badly about him.

I was expelled from that Las Vegas Middle

From Porn to the Pulpit

School, and surprisingly, Papa was not as mad as I imagined. In fact, he praised me for beating up a boy. However, he did have to send me back to Los Angeles to live with my mother. Because of my behavior I was denied admission to any other school in the Las Vegas district. So I left and headed to my mother's house.

Chapter 2

Mom, Here I Come!

I must admit that I was nervous on the way back to L.A. Although Vanessa was my mother, I didn't really know her or what I was about to get myself into. Once I arrived at her apartment in Westchester, she greeted me outside. The reunion was kind of bitter. It didn't feel as if we were mother and daughter. When I walked into the apartment, I was greeted by my stepdad and my brother. It was difficult for me because it didn't feel like they were my family. I went to my new room and sat there trying to think of something good, but all I felt was animosity. I was angry because this woman that was supposed to be my mother was

From Porn to the Pulpit

absent for most of my life. She robbed me of the dreams that daughters share with their mothers. Instead of her showing me how to be a lady, it was my father who did that. When she divorced him, she divorced me too. There were many days when I felt like a motherless child. I tried to fight my anger, but it just grew stronger. I couldn't understand how a mother could just give up her daughter and continue life as if I never existed. Yes, I was a daddy's girl, but I didn't want my mom to desert me and that's exactly what she did. It never really bothered me before because I was occupied with my dad, but it sure bothered me now!

As time went on, I felt as if I were the black sheep of the family that never really fit in with them. I hated being in that apartment, so I spent most of my days outside. We had a neighbor that lived across the street. He was a tall, older man who stayed to himself, but he was friendly. He always saw me outside alone so he offered me candy and allowed me to listen to the music in his car. I've always been a very social person, so I had no problem speaking to him. I assumed he was trying to make me feel comfortable since I was new to the

Mom, Here I Come!

neighborhood.

One day we were both outside, talking and playing games for hours. It was getting too hot to stay outside so he invited me into his apartment to watch a movie. Being young and naïve, and believing that I had a new friend, I went in. He led me straight to his bedroom because there was no television in the living room. I sat on the bed while he put a movie in. He offered me something to drink, what I thought was a soda, but whatever it was, it made me pass out. I woke up to find him on top of me. This forty-year-old man just raped me! I was only twelve years old. I had no idea how long it lasted and I just wanted it to be over. I lay under him for another five minutes until he finished.

Unremorsefully, he kissed me in the mouth and told me that I would have to come over his house every day after school and "give him some." When I regained my strength, I put on my clothes and ran across the street to my mom's apartment. I went to my room and sat there in disbelief. Tears filled my eyes, but I didn't let them fall. I wanted to tell my mom but I didn't because I was scared of him. He was a big monster-man. I had no idea what he would have done to me had I ever said anything about it. So I never told anyone. I just did what I had always done; kept silent and acted as if nothing ever happened. Furthermore, he taunted me by speaking to my mother and stepdad every morning, pretending as if he were the good neighbor. I found myself dreading to go home after school because of him.

I went through an identity crisis after that. For a while I dressed gothic and like a bum, but I was teased at school for that, so I started to dress provocatively. That rape triggered something in me and anger filled my body. I wanted to say something about what was happening to me, but I couldn't. Instead I spoke with my actions.

I became an out of control teen, doing anything I wanted to do. I just didn't care anymore. I had my first drink when I was twelve, which opened the door for many more. I started staying out as long as I could, and hanging around older girls. My mother didn't allow that to go on for too long, but I was one step ahead of her. I would come home at curfew, but when she fell asleep I jumped out of my bedroom window to be with my friends.

I was extremely disrespectful to my teachers or any kind of authority, period. I blamed adults for

Mom, Here I Come!

not realizing that something was wrong with me. How could they not see that I had been violated? I felt like I didn't have to listen to anybody; not my mom, the teachers, or the police. I got into trouble at school regularly. I had what you call a 'fighting problem' every other week I was being suspended or expelled from one school after another, for fighting or ditching.

When my mother fell asleep I stole her car whenever I wanted to go somewhere, I ran away for days at a time and got arrested. I joined a gang because the boy I liked was a *Blood*, and whenever I ran away, I would stay with him in his neighborhood. I became very familiar with all the gang members so I joined the *Bloods*. I turned into the kid that parent's wouldn't allow their children to hang out with. I became so out of control that a social worker was called in, and I was sent into a group home. They picked me up from school and drove me to a house in West L.A., where bad girls went.

My first night there was unbearable. I was the new girl so, naturally, the inmates tried me as soon as I walked in the door. I was harassed by butch lesbian girls, the food was disgusting, I had ridiculous chores to do, and I was allowed visits only twice a week. It felt like I was in prison. In order for me to leave I had to stay on good behavior, so I faked it just so I could go home. They obviously fell for it because they allowed me to leave after just a few weeks.

People thought that I was such a bad kid, but that wasn't the case at all. I was just a kid who had been molested, beaten, abandoned by her father. I was raped and was forced to see the man who did it every day. To add insult to injury, my mother and I didn't get along. Consequently, I didn't know what to do, how to deal with it, or where to go. It was unusual because this kind of behavior was not me at all. I used to be a happy, well balanced child and straight A student, but the situations that took place in my life turned me into a devastated delinquent.

I never acted like this when I lived with my dad. He was very involved with my schooling and I was happy with him. Mom only came to the school when she had to pick me up from the principal's office. My grades dropped severely and I went from being an honor roll student to earning Ds and Fs.

I had become careless and miserable, and was so

Mom, Here I Come!

displeased with the way my life was going, the only way for me to express all that rage, was through violence and disrespect towards others.

Mom didn't beat me but she kept me on punishment, which consisted of no phone, no television, no hanging out, and I couldn't sneak out anymore. She left all our bedroom doors open so that she could monitor all my activities. Luckily for me, these punishments never lasted long because I was spoiled; not by my mom, of course, but by my grandmother, Gloria, and grandfather, Tommy. Whenever I needed some motherly love I would always run to my grandma. When I needed a father figure my grandpa was always right there for me. Even though they were my mother's parents, they were the total opposites of her. My grandparents are southern, hospitable, loving Christians, and my mother is none of that. When I was with my grandparents, I felt safe and adored like I did when I was with my dad. I loved my grandparents more than anybody, and I let this be known to my, mother constantly. My grandparents always wanted to keep the peace, so they played the mediators. They wanted my mother and me to work things out, but we constantly fought with each other, both verbally and physically. I was vexed with her for not being a better mother and she was frustrated with me for being so bad and disrespectful.

One afternoon on my way home from school, I was sitting at the bus stop when a champagne colored Lexus pulled up next to me. A very handsome biracial guy got out of the car and approached me. He introduced himself as "Kye." He asked for my number, but I was so mesmerized by his good looks I didn't hear him the first time. He politely asked for my number again, and this time I heard every word. We exchanged numbers and he offered to take me home, but I preferred to ride the bus since I didn't know him. When I got home I wanted to call him, but I didn't want to seem desperate, so I put the number to the side. Later on that night the phone rang and to my surprise it was him.

He said, "Hey pretty girl, what you doin' tonight?"

"Getting ready for school." I said.

"School?! How old are you?" I assumed he was caught off guard being that I looked much older.

"I'm thirteen."

Mom, Here I Come!

"You're young, but that's okay."
"Well, how old are you?"
He said, "I'm twenty-seven."

That was older than what I was used to, but he was cute and I already liked him. He insisted that I come see him that night, so I went to my mom's room to make sure she was asleep. She was, and I went out the window.

That night Kye took me to a restaurant. After we ate, he took me home and we ended the night with a kiss. We talked every day for weeks. He told me everything I wanted to hear and I fell for him fast!

One night Kye picked me up and we went to a nightclub. I had never been to a club before so I felt a little out of place, especially because this wasn't a regular nightclub. The girls were half naked and half the men there were fat, ugly, old, and married. The other half looked like Kye; very flashy and good looking with lots of jewelry. At that point I realized that I was in a strip club. I stood against the wall as I watched the girls climb up the pole and the men spend all of their money while being mesmerized by these women. Kye wandered off and I went looking for him. I found him in a back room collecting money from two strippers. He also collected money from a few men that were there.

From Porn to the Pulpit

I told him I needed to go home. We left the club and on the ride back I wanted to ask him what he was doing back there, but I didn't. I figured he'd tell me in his own time. We ended our night and I jumped back into my bedroom window.

The next day I got out of school early, so I called Kye and he came to pick me up. He told me we had a few stops to make. We pulled up to an apartment building in South Central. He said, "I want you to go up those stairs, and a girl is gonna' hand you some money. You don't need to say nothin' to her, just get the money and come back to the car." I didn't know if I should or shouldn't do it, but I did it anyway with no questions asked. I had no idea what I was doing, but everything went as planned. Then Kye and I headed to a nice hotel located in Manhattan Beach.

The hotel room was stunning. It seemed as though I was in a fairytale, but the magic soon came to an abrupt end. Kye took some pills, and smoked several blunts of marijuana. Once he got high, he became very aggressive, and demanded sex. I was planning on sleeping with him, anyway, but not like that. He completely turned me off. The fascination that I had for him quickly faded away. I

Mom, Here I Come!

wanted him to hurry up and get off of me. When the three minutes of unpleasant sex was finally over, he took me back to my mom's house. He told me that he was going to pick me up from school every day. I wanted us to be over, but we had only just begun. A few weeks went by and we continued on with this unwanted relationship. One night he picked me up and said that we needed to talk, and I agreed. We went to another hotel in L.A, but this one wasn't nearly as nice as the other one.

Kye's words to me were, "You're young but you ain't stupid. It don't take a rocket scientist to know that I'm a pimp. That girl you got the money from the other day works for me. I get money, and it's time for you to do the same thing. I know a couple of guys who saw you that night at the club with me, and they're ready to pay. So it's time for you to grow up, and get that money for me."

I looked at him as if he had lost his mind. I said, "So you want me to have sex for money?"

"Yep!"

"Take me home right now, Kye."

"Okay, it's by choice, and never by force."

He took me home and I was relieved that we were finally done, but I was very wrong. We were nowhere near done.

A month went by and I hadn't heard or thought about Kye. I even got into a new relationship with a guy named, C.T, which also happened to be my first abusive relationship. I was now thirteen, he was eighteen, and all the neighborhood girls wanted him. He was extremely attractive and he was a bad boy. I liked him a lot but there was just one problem; he loved to hit me. We were together for only a few weeks when he hit me the first time. He slapped me in my face because I said 'hi' to one of his friends. I wasn't allowed to speak to any other guys in his presence. The next time he choked me because I confronted him for sleeping with another girl. He told me that I shouldn't worry about what he did in his spare time.

As our relationship went on, he didn't need any legitimate reason to put his hands on me; he just did it whenever he felt like it. I never fought back for fear of losing my life. I knew for a fact that he had no problem shooting anybody that made him mad. C.T was crazy. He had some severe mental issues, and was prone to snap and kill you at any moment. That's why I refused to fight him back. When he smacked me around I just wiped the

Mom, Here I Come!

blood off my mouth and walked away, but right after that, C.T would chase me down and tell me how sorry he was, and that he would never do it again. He'd end his sentence with, "I love you."

I stayed because I was living out what I grew up seeing. Daddy beat his women like this, so I knew it was only a matter of time before I was beaten by my boyfriends. No one ever told me that it wasn't right for men to beat women. Domestic violence was something that was never discussed, not in my family or at school.

I stayed with C.T and continued to go to school and carry on with my life, until I became ill. I kept vomiting, and this was rare because I never got sick. I mentioned it to a girl at school, and she asked if I was pregnant. I couldn't answer her because I really didn't know. Later that day I went to a clinic not far from my middle school in Gardena, where I was greeted by a Hispanic nurse. I told her that I wasn't feeling well and that I needed to take a pregnancy test. She sent me to the bathroom to urinate into a cup. When the test was completed, the nurse told me it was positive. I was pregnant!

My heart dropped to my knees. I was in total shock. What was I going to do with a baby? I was thirteen years old in the eighth grade with no job, no money, and my baby daddy was a twenty-seven-year-old, drug dealing pimp. Furthermore, I had a new boyfriend who would have killed me had he known that I was pregnant by someone else.

I went home and questioned whether I should call Kye or not, but I knew that I had to because he was the father of my baby. I finally built up the courage to give him a call. When he answered the phone the sound of his voice instantly irritated me. I tried to be polite by asking him how his day was going. He replied by saying, "I see that you've come to your senses. You must be ready to choose up with a real pimp and get this money?"

"No dummy, I'm calling you because I'm pregnant!"

He paused for a second and said, "Why you tellin' me? I don't have nothin' to do with that."

I screamed at him until he hung up the phone. I was so angry, my head started to hurt and I had to vomit. My mom came into the bathroom and asked if I was okay. I said "yes," then she went back into her room with her beer. A few days later Kye called and asked me to make an appointment for an

Mom, Here I Come!

abortion. He said that he would take me there and also pay for it. I knew that having an abortion was wrong, but I didn't know what else to do. I made the appointment, but when the time came, he never showed up.

Another month passed and I was now four months pregnant. Kye decided to pop up again, but this time he had a different plan. He told me to keep the baby and that we could be a family. I was shocked at what I was hearing but also happy. Later that day we agreed to see each other. I should have known that something would ruin this reunion. He picked me up and we had a pleasant day, but things took a turn for the worse when he decided to tell me his plan.

He said, "The baby was a sign for us to be together, pimping and hoeing. What kid wouldn't want their daddy to be a pimp? I will take care of you while you're pregnant, but after that, you gotta get on the track."

We were sitting in his car in front of my mom's house, so without saying a word, I opened the car door and walked into the house, not responding to his ignorance.

More time passed and it was too late to have an

abortion. I only had two options: adoption or keep my baby. After giving it a lot of thought, I decided to keep my baby. I couldn't just give my child to somebody else. I chose to have sex with Kye, and now I had to deal with the consequences. I made several attempts to tell my mom but the words never came out. I couldn't understand how I could be six months pregnant and she didn't know. I came home every day, I gained a tremendous amount of weight and she saw me vomit. My mood changed, I ate everything except dirt, and yet she didn't have a clue. That was the problem. She should have paid more attention to me, which is why I decided to have my baby. I knew that the baby would never stop loving me or stop paying attention, and I needed that.

On February 20, 2003, my mind was made up. I was definitely going to have my baby. Before going to school I stopped at the clinic I'd been going to during my pregnancy, and informed the nurse that I decided to keep my baby. I needed to start prenatal care right away. She congratulated me and told me to wait in the lobby. As I sat there I began to feel a sharp pain in the lower part of my back. I tried to ignore it but the pain grew stronger. I stood

Mom, Here I Come!

up to get the nurse and that's when my water broke. Something was wrong because it was more blood than water. The ambulance was called and I was taken to a nearby hospital in Torrance. A nurse came into my room and told me that I was going to have my baby that night. Then she asked if there was anyone that she could call to come there, and I panicked. I was not about to let her call anyone and tell them I was in labor. I snatched the I.V. out of my arm and headed for the door, but I was stopped by security, not to mention the contractions I was having. I finally cooperated and asked the nurse to call my grandmother, Gloria.

I remember lying in the hospital bed hearing the screams of the mothers in labor, and the cries of newborn babies. I closed my eyes and drifted off as I wondered if C.T might be the reason why I went into premature labor, since he beat me throughout my pregnancy. I was awakened by my grandmother's voice and she was not alone. My mother was with her. Normally, my mother would have been yelling and cursing, but not this time. She was completely silent, not a word. All she did was let the tears roll down her face. For the first time I actually had compassion for her. I didn't want to be the reason for her tears, but I was. I screamed, "I'm sorry!" I lied and told them that I didn't know I was pregnant so they wouldn't be too mad at me. My grandma' wrapped me in her arms and assured me that everything would be okay, and for the very first time I didn't believe her.

Soon after that it was time for me to push. I wasn't excited about it because the doctor told me that I was having a stillborn. I pushed about three times and there he was. But something didn't add up. He wasn't dead. He was moving! Mom said, "Oh my God, he's alive!" I reached down and picked up my one pound, two ounce son who was struggling to breathe. A doctor took him immediately out of my arms and said, "We're going to try to save him."

When my son was born that night, I begged God to let him live, but a short time later, the doctor came back into the room and said, "There's nothing more we can do. Take all the time you need with him," and handed my baby back to me. I ignored what the doctor said because my son was very much alive. He was moving, his eyes were opened, and he was breathing. My only focus was my son, nothing else mattered. It was me and him against

Mom, Here I Come!

the world, and I was the happiest teen mom ever! My dreams quickly shattered when I kissed my baby and told him that I loved him. He looked up at me and smiled, then his heart stopped beating. He died in my arms and his body grew cold. It was as if he waited to hear those words before he could leave. The pain I felt was like no other. All I could do was blame myself; I hid my pregnancy and I allowed C.T to beat me. It was my fault! That night a part of me died along with my son, who I named Samaja Kavion Williams. The pain of losing my baby outweighed the pain from the molestation, the rape, the beatings, and everything else. All I wanted was my son back, but he left me and took my heart with him.

After my mom and grandma left the hospital, I made two phone calls. The first call was to Kye. I told him that I had just given birth to our son, but he passed away.

"Dang, that's messed up, but what you tellin' me for?"

"I'm telling you because he's your son, Kye!"

He laughed and said, "He ain't my son. You and him can die!" Then he hung up.

The second call was to my dad. I told him about

From Porn to the Pulpit

Samaja and asked if he could come to the hospital, thinking that this might reunite us. We hadn't seen each other since he deserted me in Las Vegas. He told me that he couldn't come. He never gave me an explanation, nor did he show any emotion to what I just told him. That night my hatred for men rekindled. I was just so angry, and I blamed God for my son's death. As far as I was concerned, God should have killed me instead of him. After that night, life had no more meaning. A week later, on my fourteenth birthday, I was released from the hospital and went home with my mom.

Although we didn't have a good relationship, I had to give her some respect because any time something drastic happened she was right there by my side. But when I came home, things changed. All the support she gave me when I was in the hospital went out the window. Now she was angry. She yelled, screamed, and blamed me for what happened. She had her nerve! If she focused more on me, than on the liquor store, maybe none of this would have happened.

Honestly, I couldn't care less about her feelings or anybody else's. What about me? What about how I felt? I just lost my son! I hoped and dreamed that the hospital would call me one day and say that they made some kind of mistake. I wanted them to say, "Your son is not dead, he's alive and you can come get him." I imagined it as one of those *Lifetime Movie Network* kind of situations; except this was no movie. Samaja really was gone.

I wanted to die so I could be with him. I thought that if I committed suicide I would be with my son again. So I tried to kill myself numerous times by taking large amounts of pills, and slitting my wrist. I even tried to hang myself, but nothing ever worked, not even a little bit. I couldn't kill myself physically, but I tried to self-destruct in many other ways. I went into a severe depression; I refused to communicate with my family. I stopped going to school and decided to drop out of the 8th grade right before graduation. My social worker suggested that I go to counseling to help me deal with the loss of my son. I went to a few sessions, but I wanted to kill the psychologist after she gave me a white baby-doll and told me to pretend like it was Samaja. After she did that, therapy was over. I gave up on everything and everybody, including men.

Chapter 3

I'm Gay ...

And I Don't Mean

'Happy'!

I was fourteen years old when I made the decision to be with women. I was young and without understanding of a lot of things, but I was most certain about one thing. I had a pure rage for men, boys and males. The thought of the opposite sex was repugnant to me. I developed an interest in girls when I was twelve, (after the rape) but it wasn't anything serious. I had my first encounter with a female who was two years older than me. I didn't like it so I went back to boys. But after the molestation, the rape, the beatings, what my dad did to me, and the death of Samaja, all that pushed me into perversion and with full force. My lust for females grew stronger. The more men hurt me the more I desired to be with a woman. I figured if I was going to go through all of that I might as well be a lesbian, and I didn't have to worry about getting pregnant. I was also drawn to other women because of the emotional attachment, the affection that they gave. I never had that before; neither one of my parents were affectionate.

I didn't grow up around homosexuals; as a matter of fact, that subject never came up. All I knew was that men and women are supposed to be together, but why would I ever want to be with another man? They destroyed my desire for them, took my want away and pushed me toward the same sex. All they ever did was inflict pain upon me, taking my heart and stomping on it. I endured the rapes, rejection, and disrespect, but when my son died, I couldn't take another man breaking my heart. Samaja was a child that never had a chance, but in this case I considered him to be one of the

I'm Gay...And I Don't Mean 'Happy'!

boys who hurt me. All I wanted was him, but he died; he left me and he's gone forever. So no more men!

There was a sixteen-year-old girl who lived a few blocks from me in Inglewood, named "Nikki." I have no idea how we connected but I met her while I was pregnant. I knew she was gay as soon as I saw her. She was very rough and tomboyish. She wore her brother's clothes and played basketball. I liked her as a friend because she was there for me during my pregnancy. She called or came by to check on me almost every day. She always told me if I needed her she would be there. We spent a lot of time together after I lost my baby. I thought she was there for moral support, but I never suspected that she actually wanted to be with me. Finally one day, she expressed her feelings and asked me to be her girl. Without giving it much consideration, I said yes. I was suffering from postpartum depression, I had no friends, I was fighting with my family, and at that time I thought I needed her. So the "relationship" began.

Nikki and I spent a lot of time together, but we kept our relationship on the "down-low." (Women are on the down-low too.) She wasn't ready to come out to her family and neither was I. Even though they had an idea, she'd never admit to it, so we carried on in secret. We were together for a few months and I really cared for Nikki, but I wanted more. I wanted to experience the whole gay lifestyle, and see what it was all about.

I started going to all girl parties and gay and lesbian festivals in Long Beach and Hollywood. I wore rainbow belts and shoestrings to represent the gay lifestyle. I surrounded myself with drag queens and transsexuals, and some of my best friends were gay guys. Next thing I knew, everybody I was around was either gay, bisexual, or "try sexual." (They would try anything once.)

Nikki and I weren't doing so well because I'd rather be in the gay click than hang with her. She wanted to settle down and fall in love (lust), but I was just getting started. I was still trying to see where I fit, in this whole lesbian life. I didn't know if I was really gay or if I just liked Nikki, so I started messing with more and more girls. I definitely got my answer. I was involved with a few females while still being with Nikki. I didn't want to let her go, until Lexus came around.

Lexus was a childhood friend of mine; she was

I'm Gay...And I Don't Mean 'Happy'!

thirteen and I was fourteen. We met in elementary school, but when we got older we separated because she was straight and I was gay. To avoid rumors at school, the straight people didn't hang with the gays even if they were friends. We knew the rules, but in the summer of 2003 we started hanging with each other again. One day I was at her house and she started acting weird, telling me over and over again that she loved me. When it was time for me to go home she kissed me. I was freaked out because I didn't know what to do. Lexus was my friend and she was straight (at least that's what I thought). When I got home Lexus had her cousin call me and tell me that she wanted to be with me. With my mouth to the floor, I just hung up the phone. I was shocked and I didn't know what to say. When she called back I listened for hours as she told me how she felt about me. I thought about what I was going to tell Nikki because I knew I was going to leave her and all the other girls for Lexus, and that's exactly what I did.

Immediately, Lexus and I were together. We had no idea what we were doing. I just wanted someone to love and for someone to love me back, even if it was a female. She was looking for the same thing.

From Porn to the Pulpit

Lexus and I were glued to the hip and when you saw her you saw me too. We were young, dumb, and we thought we were in love. We even got each other's names tattooed. We were like the gay version of Bonnie and Clyde and had each other's back. We ran away together because her family couldn't accept the fact that she was gay. Lexus' father went to the extreme when he put a gun to her head because he didn't want her to be with me. Her parents stopped at nothing to break us up. They would send the police to my house to get her every time we were together. They actually blamed me for her decision to be gay. I tried to explain to them that I didn't make her do anything. She wanted the relationship, but since I was known for being with girls and she wasn't they were convinced that I was the one who turned her out; but it wasn't like that. The more they tried to separate us the closer we became. We announced to the world that we were going to be together regardless of what people thought about it. I was with girls before, but my relationship with Lexus was serious and nothing or no one was going to break it up.

Somehow my dad found out I was with Lexus,

which gave him a new reason to not be in my life. He hated gay people. He told me over and over again how nasty I was and that I was going to burn in hell. He didn't want anything to do with me. I told my mom that Lexus and I were together, and to my surprise she accepted it. There was no name calling, no rude remarks, just an, "Okay, if that's what you want to do." I was appalled by her response, but also happy because she gave me her support. I finally told my grandparents which was the hardest because I know that they are strict Bible believers. I thought they were going to judge me, but they didn't. They loved me unconditionally, and responded by saying, "That's between you and God. We love you no matter what you do."

Lexus and I grew stronger in our relationship. She even moved in with me at my mom's house. Even though I cared for her tremendously, there was still something missing, a void that she couldn't fill. I would lock myself in the bathroom to get away from her so I could clear my mind. I loved Lexus and hated her at the same time. I was happy and sad all at once. One day I was a lesbian, the next day I wanted to be with a guy. I didn't know who I was anymore; I was all over the place. We

From Porn to the Pulpit

fought often so Lexus decided to leave. We stayed in the relationship but couldn't live together. If I wasn't already in a bad place, my mother and I constantly bickered. There was no love there. I was searching for something that neither Lexus nor my mother could give me. So I left.

Chapter 4

Looking For Love

When I left my mom's house, I moved in with my childhood friend, "Bebe." I didn't understand how it was possible for me to live there without her mother's permission. I later found out that it was okay for me to be there because her mother rarely was. Her mom, "Dina," was a beautiful woman from Trinidad and a street hustler. She got money by any means necessary, which mainly included drug dealing and gambling.

Although Dina was a hustler, she did have a

From Porn to the Pulpit

heart, especially for me. She knew the type of relationship that my mother and I had. Eventually, Dina met my mother and told her that she wanted me to come and live with her. Without asking any questions my mother allowed Dina to take me, so Bebe and I went into the house, packed my bags and left. I was relieved and yet disappointed; relieved that Dina cared enough to take me in and hurt because my mother was so quick to give me away. That day Dina became my mother.

Arriving at their apartment in Norwalk was quite difficult for me because Bebe had a newborn son. After recently experiencing the loss of my own baby, this was definitely uncomfortable for me, but Bebe eased my pain by allowing me to care for her son as if he were my own. At times I overstepped my boundaries by not giving Bebe time with her baby, but she didn't mind. Although I took full responsibility for Bebe's son by feeding him, changing him, waking up in the middle of the night, etc., he still wasn't mine. I wanted my own baby. I wanted to feel the love I felt when I had Samaja in my arms and I expressed this to Bebe.

She said, "Well have another baby, dummy!"

"I don't have a boyfriend." I protested.

Looking For Love

"You don't need one! All you need is a dude with a penis."

We laughed, but I really took it into consideration. A few days later I told Bebe that I was serious about having another baby, so she introduced me to a Hispanic guy from her school. He and I hit it off quickly. Shortly after that we became intimate for about two months. Then I decided to take a pregnancy test and the results were negative. Being disappointed with him, I quickly moved on to the next guy; another friend of Bebe's. Within a few weeks we also became sexual. I was a little more hopeful with him because my cycle was late, and I just knew that I was pregnant. When I took the test, once again the results were negative. I got rid of that guy too. I figured if they couldn't get me pregnant, I didn't need them. I was on a mission.

Bebe told me that I was doing it the wrong way. She said, "The problem is, you're going about it all wrong. Why are you trying to get a connection with these guys? Just have sex! That's all it takes to have a baby."

She was right. I didn't need an emotional connection. In fact, I didn't even have to like them. I just needed their sperm. Any attractive guy that looked my way whether black, white, tall, short, smart, or dumb, I was on him. I was determined to have a baby. It became a priority, an everyday thing.

I had sex morning, noon, and night, wherever and with whomever; not because I was a nympho, but I just wanted a baby! I soon realized why I fought with Lexus so much, I wanted something that she could never give me. I was so desperate to recreate what I had with Samaja that I wasn't going to stop until I got it. A lot of people thought that I was obsessed with sex. They called me "boy crazy," but that wasn't the case. I didn't even like boys. I was obsessed, all right; but not with sex. I was obsessed with having a child. I continued to try and pregnant with no success. One night, a guy that I was sleeping with held me in his arms and told me that he loved me, which made my heart jump. At that moment I realized that, (a) I wasn't truly a lesbian, and (b) it wasn't just a hunger for the love of a baby that I was looking for. I was hungry for love, period; no matter where it came from. Whether it was a man, woman, or baby, I just wanted somebody to genuinely love me. I was in

Looking For Love

love with love. I was fascinated by it; I was desperate for it.

Bebe's mom decided to come home for a few days. She called me into her room and sat me down on her bed.

"What are you doing? I hear you're sleeping with the whole neighborhood. Is that true?" "Yea, but–" and she cut me off.

"Are you crazy?"

I shook my head "no." I was a little scared because Dina was quick to slap you.

"How much money you got?"

"I don't have any money."

"See that's the problem. You layin' down with these fools and you didn't get a dime. If you're gonna' act like a hoe, you might as well get paid like one. As long as you got a vagina you should never be broke."

Hearing that was like déjà vu. Kye said the same thing; now Dina said it. What was with these people? I was having sex to get pregnant, not to be a prostitute! I ignored Dina's advice and continued doing it my own way.

Meanwhile, Bebe and I went around terrorizing the neighborhood. Since Dina had legal guardianship over me Bebe was no longer my friend; she was my sister and family came first in my book. Whenever she got into an altercation with someone (which was almost every day), I was right there ready to fight on her behalf. It was funny because I preferred to make a friend rather than an enemy any day, but Bebe gave me something that I yearned for; love and acceptance. She loved and accepted me as her sister and I was willing to go to battle for her in exchange. The other teenage girls were scared of us because we were a packaged deal. You messed with one, you messed with both. Every other day, if we weren't fighting, we were getting in trouble at school, or getting beat by Dina for sneaking boys into the house. This was our routine and we had fun doing it.

Most people didn't agree with our lifestyle since Dina lived the life of a thug. She was barely home and Bebe and I were left to do whatever we pleased. I respected Dina very much because she not only hustled for herself; she hustled to provide for us too. I wasn't her biological child, but she didn't treat me any different from Bebe. She loved and cared for me just as much, and reminded me on a regular basis that I was her baby too. Not only that, Dina is just a few years older than us. She had Bebe when she was fourteen. Despite what people said, we had to give her some kind of credit. She was twenty-eight at the time and taking care of two fourteen-year-olds and her newborn grandson. We had our issues like everyone else but this was my family and I loved and cared about them very much.

Bebe got pregnant with her second child and I kept trying with no luck. As time went on, and against Dina's and Bebe's wishes, I eventually moved back with my mother. Although my mother and I didn't have the best relationship, we seemed to get along better whenever I wasn't living with her, so I hoped things would remain that way if we were in the same household. I realized that no matter how bad a parent treats a child, that child wants to be with their real parents. I had high hopes that she and I could rebuild our relationship, but I was terribly mistaken.

Once back in her house, nothing changed. We continued to argue and she still refused to accept her responsibility as a mother, which made me even more angry and defiant. I just wanted her to be my mommy, but she didn't have that desire. I envied the relationships my friends had with their mothers. They were so close and I desperately wanted that, but never got it. It got to the point where I finally accepted that my mother and I would never be what I wanted us to be. After that, I gave it no more thought. I was done.

I needed to find something to do with my time, but being fourteen doesn't allow you to do a whole lot, and my mother kept me on lockdown more often than not. Since I had to stay at home all day and night I found ways to entertain myself. I decided that since I couldn't go out and have fun, I would bring the fun to me. My passion for pregnancy rekindled and I found a way to go about it.

When my mother left for work, I met up with random guys and invited them over to hang out with me. I was taking a risk because I knew that bringing total strangers to our house wasn't the smartest thing to do. It's a real easy way for someone to kill you, but I was dedicated to having another baby, so I did it anyway. I invited multiple guys over between the ages of seventeen and twenty-five. They all knew that I was only fourteen years old, but of course pedophiles don't care about

Looking For Love

your age. When these guys came to my house, I wasn't intimate with all of them, just the ones I wanted to get pregnant by. This foolishness lasted for a few weeks until I almost got caught one day when my mother came home early from work. I was too nervous about having people come over after that, so it ended; and I was still not able to get pregnant.

My mother decided to give me my freedom back, and I was able to get out of the house again. Around that time, I often hung out with an older girl named "Kristina." She suggested that I get a fake I.D. She said I could get one in downtown L.A, so that's where I went. When I got the I.D., it had my photo and my name, but the age of twenty-three on it. The only thing that meant to me was...PARTY TIME!!! So I asked Kristina if there were any parties going on.

She said, "Yeah, there's one tonight. You wanna go?"

"Of course I do!"

She told me to get dressed and head to her house. When I got there I noticed photos of a little boy.

I asked, "Who is this?"

"He's my son."

From Porn to the Pulpit

"Where is he?"

With a sad voice she said, "In the system."

I didn't want to know why. We jumped in the car and headed to what I thought was a party, but we pulled up to a quiet house on Crenshaw and 48th Street. It clearly didn't look like a party, but I went in anyway, thinking that we were just the first to arrive. Kristina knocked on the door and a man's voice yelled, "It's open!" We walked into the well kept house where we were greeted by a tall, muscular but not so attractive, Belizean man with dreads. He introduced himself to me as "Pharaoh." Although he wasn't very attractive, he was charming and he caught my attention. In the middle of our conversation, I looked up and saw Kristina snorting lines of cocaine. Now I knew why her son was in the system. I asked her when were we going to the party. She snorted another line and said, "We're at the party." Pharaoh and I continued with our conversation while Kristina got high. I explained to him the situation with my mother so, as a "friend," he offered to let me live with him.

That next day, I went to my mother's house while she was at work, gathered my things and left again. When I arrived at Pharaoh's place he was genuinely

Looking For Love

excited to have me there. He had been living alone for quite some time. (At least, that's what he told me.) The beginning was perfect. He was an absolute gentleman. Although he was a pimp and a drug dealer, he didn't act that way towards me. I expressed to him how appreciative I was for him letting me stay in his home. He was so sweet to me and made me feel comfortable (at first). And for a short time I actually felt as though I had found love in the form of friendship and that's what I'd been wanting for so long.

Things were good for a few months until Pharaoh announced his feelings for me. He told me that he really liked me and wanted more than a friendship. He began giving me money, buying me things, cooking for me. He was doing everything to make me like him, but it didn't work. I wanted a friendship, not a relationship. Pharaoh was thirty-one, I was fourteen, he wasn't attractive, and he was yet another drug dealing pimp. I didn't want that for a boyfriend. When I expressed that to him, he wasn't happy at all.

That's when everything quickly changed. We went from always laughing and talking, to no communication whatsoever. I soon found out

From Porn to the Pulpit

Pharaoh's secret. He not only sold drugs, he consumed them as well; cocaine to be exact, and he became extremely violent every time he snorted. The first time I found out how violent he could be, was when I stepped out of the shower one day. Pharaoh busted down the bathroom door, put his hands around my throat, and forced himself on top of me, but then he realized that I was on my menstrual cycle. He said, "If you weren't bleeding, I'd take it!"

Most girls in that situation would have immediately packed up and left, but I didn't. I could have gone back to my mother's house and argued with her every day, or stay with him and work it out. I chose to stay, but it only got worse. Pharaoh started bringing different prostitutes into the house. He would have sex with his bedroom door wide open, making sure I saw and heard them. He started snorting more and more cocaine, drinking, smoking weed, and being more violent. The hits came more often. He would find reasons to fight me, especially at night when he was in the mood for sex.

Although he was treating me like dirt, I still cared for him. When he became sick from overindulging in his drugs and alcohol, I would fix him tea or food to make him feel better. He showed his appreciation by hitting me and calling me obscene names. One day, when he wanted me to have sex with him once again, I refused as always, and this time he punched me in the face and dragged me to the bedroom by my hair. Then he kicked, slapped, and punched me some more. I don't know where I got the strength, but I got up off the floor and fought back! I was tired of him beating on me for no reason.

It was like that scene in the movie, **"What's Love Got To Do With It,"** where Tina Turner fought Ike in the limo. But the more I fought back, the angrier Pharaoh got. He dragged me into the bathroom and slammed my head on the edge of the bathtub. I laid there for a moment in agonizing pain. It scared Pharaoh because he thought I was dead. When I opened my eyes and saw that his face was just as bloody and bruised as mine, I smiled. He cleaned his face and left the house. A few minutes later there was a knock at the door. During my stay at Pharaoh's house, I found myself meeting all kinds of people; strippers to be exact. There was one stripper in particular by the name of "Diamond."

From Porn to the Pulpit

She bought weed and cocaine from Pharaoh at least once a week. Although she had a drug habit, she was a really sweet girl. She hated how Pharaoh treated, so when she walked through the door and saw my bloody face, she said, "Oh no! He did this to you?" I shook my head yes, while I wiped the blood from my nose.

"Why are you still here? You need to get your own place and get away from this idiot."

"Where am I gonna go, Diamond? I don't have any money."

She looked at me and said, "Well, you wanna be grown, you gotta' get paid like you're grown. Come with me to the after hour tonight, so you can get enough money to get out of here."

As I sat there with my mind wondering, I came to the conclusion that maybe, just maybe, I should strip. After all, I did hear it from Kye, Dina, and now Diamond. I desperately needed to get away from Pharaoh. So tonight was the night.

Chapter 5

The

Beginning of Disaster

Hours later, Diamond was ready to go to the after hour. I didn't know what to wear to a place like that, so I asked for her advice. Her response was, "Look like a hoe as much as possible." Since I had no "hoe attire" she gave me a mini-skirt and a strapless top to wear.

The drive up there was too much for me to bare. I had knots in my stomach. Diamond gave me instructions on what to do once we arrived. She told me to follow her straight to the back, and don't stop to talk to anybody until we got dressed. Once

From Porn to the Pulpit

we got to the back room, Diamond put a lot of makeup on my face to cover the bruises Pharaoh left. Then, she pulled out a red bikini and a pair of black, six-inch heels and told me to put them on. I asked her where were we supposed to get dressed. She said, "Right here." I was so shy, I didn't want to take my clothes off in front of the other girls, but I did. As I undressed, I worried that one of the strippers would realize that I was underage, but that didn't happen, mainly because most of them were in the corner getting high. I was almost in my comfort zone until a guy walked in, and slapped one of the strippers. I figured he must have been her pimp. Diamond whispered in my ear, and told me to hurry up, so we could get out of there.

Once I got dressed it was time to go on stage. When I walked out there, half naked in front of all those men, I immediately turned back around and ran into the dressing room. Diamond followed me and said "Girl, what's wrong with you?" I told her I couldn't do it. I was so nervous my hands were sweating and my legs were shaking. She told me to relax. Then, she handed me a glass of Gin and put a blunt to my lips. I drank as fast as I could and smoked as much as my lungs could handle. The

The Beginning of Disaster

weed and alcohol quickly calmed my nerves and it was now time for me to go back on stage.

My heart was beating a million miles a minute, so I took another drink and a deep breath. When I got on stage I danced with my back towards the crowd, pretending as if no one was there. Every time I attempted to face them, I couldn't. Being in six-inch stilettos didn't help either. Then, all the guys started to surround the stage to put money in my bikini. Their touch made my body tense, but the more money I saw, the easier it got. I danced for approximately nine minutes, but it seemed like an eternity.

As I attempted to leave the stage, a few men requested lap dances. Their propositions were extremely uncomfortable because I could see they were becoming aroused. I didn't know what to do. I just continued to dance nervously, as they whispered perverted things in my ear. While they rubbed their hands all over my body, different thoughts entered my mind. I wondered if I was older or younger than their daughters. It seemed as though the whole time I was out there I held my breath, and when it was all over, I could finally breathe again. Diamond and I were at this strip club for about an hour, and then we left.

On the way back to Pharaoh's house, I was drenched with the smell of alcohol and cigarette smoke. Diamond congratulated me, and told me how proud she was of me. Before I got out of her car I counted the money. It was over two hundred dollars, and I was ecstatic! I made two hundred dollars in a matter of minutes, just from dancing! It was a wrap. I found my new career. I'm going to be a stripper!

I still had my fake I.D, which meant I could go to any strip club I wanted to. I went to another club in Los Angeles, and the manager liked what he saw. He hired me on the spot, and asked me for my stage name. At the after hour, everyone called me "Lil Bit," because of my petite size, but I wanted something else; something grown and sexy, something that people would remember. Just then it came to me. Daddy used to call me his "Little Queen." So that's the name I went with, "Queen." Sometimes, depending on how I felt, I added the "B" on the end.

The stripper lifestyle wasn't an easy thing for me at first. I was only fourteen years old, dancing in a grown woman's pair of shoes. No matter how

The Beginning of Disaster

grown I wanted to be, I was just a kid. I was surrounded every night by grown men and women, pretending like I knew what they were talking about, but I really had no clue. I always worried that someone would find out my real age. Things became even more complicated when I found out most of the strippers were drug addicts. I was taken back when I saw these beautiful women pumping hard drugs into their systems. I couldn't see how dancing would make them want to get high. (I soon found out.) I've never seen so much drug use in my life. The dressing room was their drug domain. After leaving the stage, the girls ran back there to get a hit. The customer's fantasy girl was really a dope fiend.

There were three types of strippers: the college students who planned to get enough money to pay for school, but got comfortable with the fast money, and eventually forgot all about school. The single mothers, who had to take care of their children without the help of the fathers. The rest didn't know what else to do with their lives, so they decided to dance until they figured it out. I fell into this third category because I didn't know what I was doing. I really didn't have a plan; I was just infatuated with the fast money. I also found out that the strip club was not a place for you to make friends. It was a competition. Every girl was competing with each other for a dollar.

Money was coming in like crazy, because I was the new kid on the block. Men like new things, and since I was new I made more money, which meant more problems…with the girls, that is. One major rule that one should never break in the strip club is never steal a girl's customer. If one guy is paying a certain girl, he was considered "her regular," and he was off limits. Ask me if I cared about that rule, or any other rules? When I was in the club, I was like a lion, and the customer was my prey! The other strippers couldn't stand me, which caused a whole lot of fights. I wasn't bothered by it because I was used to it, but to have to fight in the club, then go home and fight Pharaoh, was becoming too stressful. I decided to continue dancing; just at another club.

I made sure I informed Pharaoh immediately about my decision. To avoid extra conflict I had to tell him everything. When I walked into the house, he was sitting at the table snorting a line of cocaine.

He said, "Where' you been?"

The Beginning of Disaster

"I was at the club."

"How much money did you make?"

"Why? You wanna' pimp me too?"

(That was a big mistake.) He cursed at me for a few minutes, and then he got up from the table with a gun in his hand. He said, "Do you think you can do whatever you want in my house?"

Before I could answer he hit me in my face, and pulled the trigger. The gun went off, and the first shot went right past me into the wall. I was so frightened that I urinated on myself. Pharaoh walked up to me, and put the gun in my face, and with confidence he said, "This time I won't miss." He pulled the trigger the second time, but the gun jammed. He stood there for a moment trying to get the gun to work, but it didn't. After that I had had enough. When he went into the bathroom I ran out of the house. I sat in Leimert Park for hours thinking about my next move. I decided to go to my grandparents' house in Compton. I couldn't take the abuse from Pharaoh any longer.

I went to my grandparents' house where I was always welcomed and my mother happened to be there too. When they saw my face they panicked right away. They asked what happened, but I made up a story, so Pharaoh wouldn't get in trouble. They continued to question me, but I stuck to my story. My mother placed an icepack on my face. It was funny how the only time we bonded was during tragedy. It was as if she was reminding me that she was still my mother and I was still her daughter, despite our differences. Although that day was devastating for me, it was actually the beginning of a new love between my mother and I. However, I still didn't want to live with her, so I called Diamond and asked her to come pick me up.

When she arrived, she told me I could stay with her until I got enough money to get my own place. I continued dancing at bachelor parties, after hours, and private parties for a while. Everything was fine until I met "Toni." tragedy.

Toni was a very handsome drug dealer whom I met at an after hour. He sat at the bar ordering Hennessey and Coke while he watched me dance. He asked for my number, we talked on the phone a few times, and I became interested in him. One day, Tony called and asked if I could take a day off from work so that we could spend some time together, but I said no. Although I liked him, I liked money more. He told me he would give me five hundred

The Beginning of Disaster

dollars if I skipped work. At that point, my schedule opened up and I met him at a motel near L.A.X Airport.

When I walked into the room I could tell the vibe was different. He handed me the money and said, "We need to talk, but not here. Let's take a ride." I was confused, but I agreed to go. Then, he went into the bathroom for a long period of time and when he finally came out, he had white powder on his nose and his eyes were blood shot red. Instantly, I copped an attitude. It was déjà vu; first Kye, then Pharaoh, now Tony. I kept ending up with drug addicts. I knew this night would only get worse.

We left the motel and drove to the Hollywood Park Casino in Inglewood. We pulled into the parking lot, and I asked him what were we doing there. He told me to go into the casino and, "Get a few dates. When you're finished bring me back the money."

I laughed and asked him if he was serious. He slapped me in my mouth, busting my lip, and with a stern voice he said, "Do you think I'm serious now? Go in there, find some dudes, take them to the bathroom, the car, wherever! Just get the money and give it to me!" I looked at him in disbelief because I didn't see this coming. I told him I was not going to do that. He hit me again, and in his frustration we left the casino.

On the way back to the motel, he told me that he was going to kill me, and everyone in my family. I tried to run to my car, but Tony grabbed me by my throat and dragged me to his room. He told me to take my clothes off and when I said no, he slapped me on the bed and said, "I'll take 'em off for you!" Then, he forced himself on top of me. I buried my face in the pillow, so he couldn't hear me scream due to the throbbing pain I suffered from him roughly jamming his large penis inside of me. The room was dark, so he couldn't see my tears. I laid there lifeless and took it as he whispered in my ear, "Daddy just wants you to be a good girl." When he finished he told me to get out.

The ride home was very uncomfortable for me. I was in so much pain I could barely close my legs. I took a bath hoping that would soothe the pain, but it didn't help much. I wasn't just hurting physically, but mentally and emotionally as well as I endured yet another rape. I went into the kitchen and drank a fifth of gin, then passed out on the floor. The next day I woke up in my own vomit. I was in physical

The Beginning of Disaster

and emotional pain, more so emotional because I liked Tony, and I couldn't understand why he and Pharaoh did these things to me. I was just fourteen years old and tired of this game already. I needed a break. I left Diamond's apartment, and went to my grandparents' house.

I moved in with my grandparents, which was a good idea because I got back on the right track. I stopped dancing, went back to school and stayed out of trouble for a while (a short while). I wasn't drinking and hanging out with the wrong people, I was on top of my school work, and Lexus and I got back together. I started respecting my mother too. I even got a job at L.A.X Airport. I really did try to do the right thing.

I grew a lot closer to my grandparents and we had a remarkable relationship, but I didn't want to be there either. They had too many rules. They wanted me to go to school, come straight home, and do homework. If I wanted to go outside I had to be in the house before the street lights came on. Lexus could only come over on the weekends and I had to be in bed by 9:00 P.M., and so on. Obviously, I wasn't feeling that at all. I had experienced freedom, living without guardianship, and adulthood at the age of fourteen, and I wasn't ready to give that up. I just couldn't get used to the square life.

In the mean time I stayed busy with church. That was the only place my grandparents would allow me to go without any restrictions. No matter what day or time, as long as I was in church they were fine with it. I grew up in a Baptist church and I actually enjoyed being there. It was the one thing in my life that always went right. I accepted Jesus as my personal Savior at a very young age and was baptized at the age of thirteen. I spent a lot of time in Sunday school, Bible study, youth church, and also sang in the choir. A girl named "Natalie" sung in the choir with me and we became really good friends. I admired her because of her zeal for God and her love for the choir. Every time I saw her she had a big smile on her face and I trusted her because we shared the same secret. We had both danced before.

I was now fifteen and Natalie had just turned eighteen. My grandparents trusted me with her because she was a church girl (or so they thought). We started spending a lot of time together in and out of church. She knew that I didn't really want to

The Beginning Of Disaster

be at my grandparents' house because of all their rules, so one day she called and said I could live with her in the San Fernando Valley. She also said we could start dancing together! Immediately, I packed my bags and once again, I left.

Chapter 6

Pimps & Prostitutes

When you're a stripper you come across a lot of different people; married men, doctors, lawyers, hustlers, drug dealers, but most of all pimps and prostitutes. Every club has them. Most people think that every prostitute is a stripper, and that every stripper is a prostitute, but that's not true. A lot of girls, like me, strip but don't have sex for money. Other girls have sex for money, but don't strip, and some do both. The pimps in the club are there for one of two reasons; they are either watching the girls they already have, or trying to recruit new ones. I knew all about the game, but that wasn't my thing. I wanted to dance and that's it. But Natalie changed all of that. When she picked me from my grandparents' house, we drove to her three bedroom condo in the Valley. It was very luxurious; she had two cars, a poodle, fancy furniture, and a lot of brand name clothes. Like the devil, she offered me the same thing, but I had to pay a price. In our conversation she told me plain as day, that dancing was not going to get me anywhere.

She said, "If you want some real money, then you gotta spread your wings."

Looking dumbfounded, I asked her what did that mean.

"Danielle, you're a pretty girl, and I see you got some money from dancing in the club, but you're not even getting half of what I get. It's not because I'm better than you or nothin' like that. I just go hard and you don't."

With an attitude I said, "What do you mean by that?"

She grabbed my vagina and said, "Money and power are between your legs! I see how you operate. Dudes come around and whoever you like, you try to be their girlfriend, and it makes me laugh! Do you actually think they're gonna wife

Pimps & Prostitutes

you? If you put more effort into getting money from them instead of falling in love, you'll be alright."

I said, sarcastically, "So if a guy offers me money I'm supposed to take it and sleep with him? You want me to be a hoe?"

"Lil mama, you're already a hoe in their eyes, just by being a stripper! All you gotta do is give them a price. If they agree, take the money, go to a hotel or wherever you're comfortable, do your thing and get on. It's that simple. The only difference is, you're gettin paid for something you been doing for free. I'm just sayin' why make four or five hundred dollars a night, when you can make four or five thousand dollars a night?"

I was a little shocked that my choir member from the Baptist church I grew up in was introducing me to prostitution. It's bad enough that I danced for money, but now Sister Natalie from the church wants me to sell my goods. This was definitely not the same girl I was singing about Jesus with.

The strange thing was, the more she explained it to me the better it started to sound. Why did I care about these men? They didn't care about me. They rape me, beat me, abandon me, and everything else. She's right. I am stupid for caring and the more I thought about the pain that men caused me, the angrier I got. So, now it's my turn! Every man t h a t comes my way will have to pay; literally. This even pushed me back to being with women, permanently. Men broke my heart, so now I'm going to break their pockets. Natalie painted a pretty picture, and like a fool, I fell for it. I agreed to prostitute myself with my choir member from my church.

Once I agreed, Natalie was so excited. She starting unpacking my things and putting them into her closet. She turned up the music and poured me drink after drink. Then a man walked through the door. Natalie told me he was her boyfriend. She must have thought that I was an idiot. I knew for sure he was not her boyfriend. That man was her pimp, which made me upset because this was her first lie. To my surprise, there were many more to come. Being very drunk, I paid little attention to the boyfriend/pimp.

Natalie grabbed my hand and said, "Are you ready?"

I wanted to scream NO!!! But foolishly I said yes.

"Alright, let's go."

Pimps & Prostitutes

We went to a hotel in Sherman Oaks. On the way up the stairs she said, "Relax and pay attention. Don't worry about nothin'. I got you." I drank another shot of gin that I had in my purse from earlier, and followed her into the nice hotel suite. A heavy-set, older Caucasian man was sitting on the bed. He got up, hugged Natalie and said, "Oh you brought a friend?"

"Yeah, this is my girl, Queen. She's pretty, huh?"

Biting his lip and shaking his head, he said, "Oh yeah, she's beautiful."

I wanted to throw up, and not because I was drunk. Then, Natalie said to him, "So how much are you gonna' pay for the both of us?"

"I don't have much money on me, but I can give you five hundred a piece and some weed."

Natalie agreed and he went into the bathroom. She whispered in my ear and said, "Don't trip. It'll be over in five minutes, literally."

Nervously, I said okay and took another drink. He came out of the bathroom and said, "Alright ladies, let's get this show on the road!"

He undressed and lay on the bed, Natalie and I joined him. His touch paralyzed my body. I was unable to move or even breathe for a second. I didn't know if I was disgusted from seeing his big, fat, unattractive body, or if I was in shock by what was happening. I tried to get involved, but I couldn't. I tried to touch him, but my hand wouldn't move. My brain told my body what to do, but it didn't listen. I felt like I was in the twilight zone. When Natalie saw my condition, she took over and put his attention on her. It only lasted for seven minutes, but that seven minutes felt like seven hours.

When it was over he thanked us and told Natalie to get the money out of his wallet. She got it and we left. In the car she handed me five hundred dollars and said, "Don't worry lil' mama; you'll be okay. I know it's hard the first time, but just keep drinking."

I couldn't believe how fast we got that money. Although that experience was hard for me, I wanted more. I asked her if she knew anybody else we could go see. She went through her cell phone and called another guy.

"Hey baby, what you doin'? I'm coming over and I have a friend with me."

She hung up and said, "He's real cool. He's an older, retired black dude. His wife died and left him a whole lot of money. We're gonna do the same thing, but he's gonna give us more than five hundred a piece."

We pulled up to a mini mansion not far from the hotel we had just left. I was so drunk I could barely walk. Natalie helped me out of the car and said, "Pull yourself together; don't nobody want a sloppy hoe!"

We walked into the unlocked house and found the old man standing in his kitchen making a drink. Natalie hugged him and introduced me to him.

He said to Natalie, "Girl, you sure know how to pick 'em." He slapped me on my behind and said, "I like you."

I smiled cunningly. I didn't want him to touch me I just wanted his money. We sat on his couch and Natalie said, "How much do you have to play with both of us?

"How much do you want?"

"Eight hundred a piece."

My eyes popped out of my head. I just knew he wasn't going to give us that much.

He said, "Not a problem, baby girl."

He went into the back room and came back handing us eight hundred dollars each. I wanted to scream. Natalie asked me if I was ready, I said, "Yeah." She whispered in my ear and said, "He's easy to deal with. I'll do most of the work. All you have to do is pretend like you like him."

I thought it would be easier the second time around, but it was just as difficult as before. We stayed for another fifteen minutes and then we left.

On the way home the alcohol started to wear off, and I was feeling disturbed by what had just happened. I looked at Natalie and said "Does it get easier?"

She said, "It will get easier as time goes by."

"So you're used to doing this?"

She looked me in my eyes and said, "You'll never get used to it, you just learn to deal with it."

"But how do you deal with sleeping with all those men night after night?"

She said, "I try not to think about it, I just do it. And plus I do drugs, a lot of drugs, to keep my mind off of it."

After that, we both sat in a weird silence on the way home, as our minds wandered off. It was five in the morning when we got home. The sun was just coming up, but I was wide awake. I sat on the bedroom floor and poured out all the money. I made five hundred dollars from the white guy and eight hundred from the black guy. I made thirteen hundred dollars in one hour between two men. I fell in love with money and wanted more.

Although the money was staring me in the face, I couldn't shake the feeling of disgust and humiliation from what I had done to get it. My emotions got the best of me. I curled up into a fetal position next to the money with tears in my eyes. The first thing that came out of my mouth was, "God, I'm so sorry. Please forgive me."

Natalie walked in and asked what was wrong, but before I could tell her she said, "You trippin' about what happened? I should've told you it would be a little uncomfortable the first time, but hold on, I got something for you." She went for her purse and came back to my room with weed. We started smoking but I told her that I wasn't a big fan of marijuana. So she reached into her purse again and pulled out a bag with white powder. I knew what cocaine looked like, but this stuff looked different. Natalie told me it was crystal meth. She poured it on a handheld mirror, and sniffed it with a rolled up dollar bill. Then it was my turn. I was skeptical about doing hard drugs, but I needed something to kill that feeling of shame and discomfort. So I sniffed the crystal meth and it felt like my nose was on fire. I sat there with Patron in my cup, and drifted off as the drugs took over my body, hoping the emotional pain would soon go away.

After that night, Natalie and I became inseparable for several months, until she got arrested and went to jail for prostitution. She never told me that she had warrants, so when the police caught her, she had to serve a year. I didn't know what to do then. She was my partner; we were like *"Thelma and Louise."* The following day she called me collect from jail and I told her that I was miserable because I couldn't get money without her.

She yelled at me and said, "What's wrong with you? You can get money, you don't need me! You should be happy now; you can get more money when you're by yourself. You don't have to split it with nobody! I showed you what to do, now go get it. You can do it!"

After talking to her, I realized that I didn't have any other choice; I had to do it by myself. I was comfortable with Natalie because she would do

Pimps & Prostitutes

most of the work, while I did little or nothing. I never had actual intercourse with those men, she did it for me. Now I had to step my game up. I decided to work "the track" by myself for the first time. (The track is a street where prostitutes work.) I didn't have a car anymore, so I took the bus, and the whole ride there was nerve racking. I dressed in jeans and a T-shirt, so I wouldn't draw attention to myself, but I had a mini-skirt, a wig, and some heels in my bag. My mind was all over the place as I thought about what I was getting ready to engage in. The ironic thing about it was when I was younger, my friends and I would harass and rob prostitutes while they were on the track. I had become the very thing I despised. After the long bus ride, I went into a nearby *Jack in the Box* and changed my clothes in the bathroom. I really didn't know what to do because the track wasn't our style. We had clients that we went to, but they were Natalie's clients. Now I needed clients of my own and I had to start somewhere.

   I headed to Sepulveda, a well known street where prostitutes work. I was out there for about fifteen minutes when the first car pulled up. He was a middle-aged Armenian man, in a silver Range

From Porn to the Pulpit

Rover. I was so petrified, my hands started shaking uncontrollably, and I couldn't open the passenger door. He leaned over and opened it for me, I got in and he drove off. We stopped at his bank, and he asked if I was hungry. I never turn down food so I accepted. He took me to dinner at a nice restaurant on Ventura Blvd. I didn't expect this kind of treatment, especially since he picked me up off of the street, but I guess he wanted to feel like he wasn't with a prostitute. When we finished eating, we headed back to his place in Woodland Hills. He lived in a nice condo and mentioned something about his law firm, so he definitely had money. We sat on his couch and he said, "This is my first time doing anything like this." I wanted to say, "Mine too!" But I didn't want him to know that I was just as nervous as he was. We drank some wine, and I made sure I was tipsy. He leaned over to kiss me, but I turned my face. I never allowed those men to kiss me; that was too personal. Not to mention, I didn't know if they brushed their teeth regularly. He apologized and handed me the money. I turned all the lights off as I undressed because I didn't want to look at him. When he got on top of me, my body tensed up. I tried to imagine him as someone else, but that didn't work, my body was still rejecting him. I thought about the money he just gave me, which quickly relaxed me. In the middle of us having sex, the wine wore off. I looked at him and suddenly realized what I was actually doing. The thought of me having sex with this stranger who just picked me up off the street was disgraceful. Without saying a word, I just let the silent tears roll down my face. When it was over, he dropped me off on the same corner he picked me up from. I didn't have the energy to sleep with anybody else that night, so I headed home and jumped in the shower. I could smell his scent on me. I scrubbed my body continuously, until it started to hurt. The experience of turning my first trick was just as traumatic and soul-shattering as I had always imagined, but I couldn't stop. It was just the beginning.

When I got the courage to go back on the streets, I was intrigued by the men that I met. When you think of a client, a customer, a john, a trick, or whatever term you want to use, you think of an old, weird, fat, loser kind of guy; but that's not the case in most situations. The type of men that picked me up were very professional. They were doctors, lawyers, musicians, photographers, and so on. Ninety-five percent of them were married and they showed me pictures of their wives and children. Some of them were bold enough to bring me in their homes while their wives were at work or on vacation. I was also picked up by virgins who wanted to lose their virginity with no strings attached.

The thing that really surprised me was most of the men were in the church, but had very disturbing sexual needs. When the Pastors and Deacons picked me up, I thought they wanted to pray for me and help me to stop prostituting. Instead, they paid me to for sex! I discovered a great deal about my clients' personal lives during our conversations. They didn't just pick me up for sex. They conversed with me about their marriages, kids, finances, careers, etc. The job was not at all how I imagined. Dare I say, it had perhaps a "human side?" I thought they would pick me up, pay for sex and drop me off at the corner. After all, it was "the track," but they didn't do that. I kind of wished that it was just sex and money, because I couldn't care less about their personal problems, their fears, and fantasies.

Pimps & Prostitutes

The following night I was on Sepulveda working the track again, when the first guy pulled up. I got into his car and within minutes the police pulled up behind us. It was vice night, and all the undercover officers were waiting to take people to jail. I was really frightened and I didn't know what to do. I couldn't say he was my boyfriend because he was Latino and didn't speak very much English. Not only that, I was only fifteen years old! A female cop came to my window and told me to get out of the car. Before I could make up a lie, the guy started crying and admitted that he picked me up for sex. They handcuffed me and took me to the station. I was astonished when they gave me a paper to sign saying if it happens again they can take further action or something to that extent. I was so relieved when they let me go with just a warning.

Instead of using my brain, I went right back to Sepulveda that next night. I jumped in the car with a Caucasian man, and the same female police officer from the night before stopped us. She laughed as she arrested me again and said, "You just couldn't wait, huh?" She put me in the police car and we headed for the station, but this time when I got there, I didn't leave. Since I was underage I gave them a fake name and birthday. They booked me and put me in a cell with not only prostitutes, but crack addicts, thieves, and psychotic, crazy women who were in there for all kinds of crimes. The temperature was ridiculously cold and the odor was horrendous. It smelled like death. I lost at least seven pounds because I refused to eat the detestable food. I was locked up from Thursday until Monday, and in all that time, I withheld my bladder and bowels because I disallowed myself to sit on the same toilet as the rest of the inmates. When I finally went to court and stood before the judge, thankfully, he let me go. If things weren't bad enough, as soon as I was released, Lexus called me. She decided that she didn't want to be with me anymore. We were both cheating on each other; the only difference was that I was getting paid, but she gave her heart to someone else. I was devastated and my heart was broken but I couldn't blame her because I put her through a lot. I wouldn't want to be with an emotionally, unstable prostitute either.

When Lexus left, I got involved with an older woman named, Violet. I met her at a gay club in L.A. She was twenty years my senior and the

Pimps & Prostitutes

daughter of an Apostle. We were together for a few months, when we decided to move in with each other. She accepted the fact that I was a dancer, but I knew she would never be with me if she knew I was prostituting, so I took a break from prostitution and went back to the club to dance.

I had a strong dislike for pimps because of my experiences with Kye, Pharaoh, and Tony, so I kept my distance from the ones in the club. However, there was one guy named "S.D" that all the girls wanted. I knew he was a pimp, but he was different from the rest. I guess I had the right outfit on that night, because when I got on stage, S.D threw a large amount of money at me, smiled, and walked away. When I finished dancing I walked over to thank him for the money. He said, "You're welcome." And then he brushed me off. Shockingly, it made me even more interested in him. A man never brushed me off before, especially not in a club. This was definitely different and I liked it.

I carried on with my night and every once in a while I'd glance over at S.D and he would look back at me and wink. This went on for a couple of nights. We both acted uninterested in each other when that obviously wasn't the case. He got tired of playing that game, so he asked me to join him after the club. Despite my past experiences with the other pimps, I accepted. We went to his tattoo shop in Inglewood and slept together that night. After that I was hooked. I stayed with him for three days straight. Violet was very upset because I didn't call or come home. It was funny because I thought I didn't like men at all, but this man made me feel so superb. I didn't know what it was about him but when I was in his world, he was my king and I was his queen. Unfortunately, he didn't want to be my king; he wanted to be my pimp.

The third night we were together, he said we needed to talk. I already knew where this was going. As he talked, he promised me the world. He told me about all the money we could make together, and blah, blah, blah. I had already heard this mess before, but when I said no, there was always a consequence. I just didn't know how severe his was going to be. When I told him I didn't want to be his prostitute, I was blown away when he said, "Okay," and kissed me on my forehead. This had to be a joke. He didn't slap me, beat me, stab me, or anything! Sadly, I was expecting him to

Pimps & Prostitutes

do something to me, but he didn't. He just laid there next me and held me, until we fell asleep.

S.D and I continued our relationship, making it known to everyone that he was my man and I was his woman. Actually I wasn't his woman, I was his girl, because I just turned sixteen and he was in his forties; but I didn't care. I was in lust. S.D spoiled me, he made time for me, and I wasn't just a stripper to him. We had genuine feelings for each other. He taught me the dos and don'ts of the game. He even taught me how to get more money from men. S.D showed me how to be sexy. Although I had a pretty face, I had no sex appeal. He called me a "Pretty Thug" because I still behaved like a gang banger. In a weird way he was like a father figure. He was older, he was my provider, and he was everything that I needed him to be.

The other strippers couldn't stand me even more because I had who they wanted. One night a stripper named, "Secret" came up to me and said, "I don't know why you braggin' about him. He's married. He's just using you, stupid!" I called her a few names and tried to hit her with a bottle but before it got out of control I caught myself. I ignored her because twenty-three hours of the day

From Porn to the Pulpit

she high and she also like S.D, so I didn't pay her much attention. However, as the night went on, what she said started to bother me, so I asked S.D if it was true. He responded with a straight face and said, "Yeah I'm married; so what?"

I wanted to slap him, but I just walked away furious. He grabbed me and said, "Why you trippin'? You worried about the wrong thing. So what; I'm married! I'm always with you, so what's the problem?"

"What do you mean, you're married, fool! You should've told me that, instead of me hearing it from somebody else."

He smiled and kissed me on my forehead. Then he opened the car door and told me to get in. As bad as I wanted to walk away, I just couldn't resist him and he knew it. This man had a hold on me. We had a super soul tie. I was well aware that sleeping with a married man was wrong, but all my morals went out the door when it came to S.D. He was right. We were together all the time, so why should I worry about him being married or being a pimp? I wanted him and everything that came along with him.

A year passed and S.D and I were still together.

Pimps & Prostitutes

He wasn't worried about Violet and I wasn't worried about his wife. His wife scared away all his other women by beating them up, but the two of us never crossed those roads, but if we ever did I was just as ready as she was. As far as I was concerned, S.D was mine. He was good to me and took care of me in every way. It wasn't all about the money. He made me feel like I was his wife. S.D wasn't your average pimp, or maybe he just really did care for me. He treated me so differently from the other women in his life. He made me feel special, but once again, it didn't last long.

One day I got a phone call and he didn't sound like himself. I knew something was wrong because he told me that he loved me. S.D showed me love, but he never actually said it. So I knew something wasn't right.

He said, "I love you, and I have fun when I'm with you, but I made a vow to my wife and what I'm doing with you ain't right. It would be different if you worked for me because it would be all business, not personal. My wife doesn't deserve this. I never gave our marriage a chance. It was a hard decision but I had to choose, and since she married me, I could at least give our marriage a try, and that's what I'm going to do. So you and me are done. I'm sorry."

He had just turned forty-five, so I figured he was going through a midlife crisis or something. I said, "That's not fair to you or me, and your marriage is a joke. You're gonna force yourself to be happy with her when you know you really wanna be with me? S.D don't do this, I love you!"

He said, "I love you too." And then he hung up.

I called him repeatedly, until he turned his phone off and I couldn't get through. I laid in my bed and not even Gin or Patron could numb me from the pain I felt. I cried so hard I gave myself a headache. I was sixteen years old and in lust with a forty-five year old married pimp. It really hurt me because I didn't care for men in that way, but I let my guard down with him. I allowed him into my heart. I even risked my relationship with Violet to be with him. I felt so stupid to think that he would actually leave his wife for me. My little heart was broken, and I dealt with it by drinking a fifth of Gin and cranberry juice.

I went to the club expecting to see him there, but he didn't show up that night, or the next night, or

Pimps & Prostitutes

the one after that. Soon a week turned into a month and he still didn't show up, which was unusual because the club was S.D's everyday hangout spot.

A month passed and we didn't talk or see each other. I accepted that we were really over, so it was back to normal. I continued my relationship with Violet, and men were used for business purposes only. S.D was the last man that I ever gave my heart to and I made sure this never happened again. My hatred for men just increased.

While dancing at a bachelor party, I met a prostitute named, "Honey." We talked all night and exchanged numbers. The next day she called and asked what my plans were for that night and I told her I was getting ready to go to the club.

She said, "Forget the club! This white dude I know got a lot of money, and when I say a lot, I mean a whole lot. He calls me every once in a while, and he called me today. I told him I had a friend and he wants both of us to come over. He's gonna give us twelve hundred each for an hour!"

She gave me his address and I met her in Encino. I pulled up to a gorgeous mansion. This man was obviously a celebrity or something. His maid opened the door and we walked past six bedrooms

From Porn to the Pulpit

to get to the living room where he was. He gave Honey a hug and said, "Who's your friend?"

I quickly responded and said, "Hello, my name is Queen. It's nice to meet you."

He smiled and looked at my feet. "You have amazing feet, can I touch them?"

It was so awkward, but I said yes. We sat on his couch and he took my heels off, I asked what he did for a living and he said, "I'm a retired baseball player. I used to play for the Dodgers years ago." I complimented his beautiful home; he thanked me and walked toward the kitchen. Honey told me he was weird. He had a foot fetish and paid a lot of money to get freaky with your feet. He must have liked my feet a whole lot because he came back to the living room and told Honey to go to the other side of the house to get something. When she left, he handed me fifteen hundred dollars and told me to put my number in his phone, "But don't tell Honey."

When she came back, he told us to walk around his mansion barefoot. This turned him on and it turned me off. It was so strange, but this was just the beginning of all the weird fetishes to come. Two days later he called me and asked if I could come

Pimps & Prostitutes

by myself. When he heard the hesitation in my voice, he offered to give me another fifteen hundred dollars. That's all he had to say. I went over there and he became my regular.

I accepted that I was a prostitute, but deep down inside I really didn't want to do it. I was infatuated with the movie *Pretty Woman*, hoping that would be my story one day, too.

One night I was low on cash, so without Violet's knowledge I decided to work on the track. A gorgeous black man pulled up in a brand new, white Cadillac Escalade. I was a little indecisive, because one of the rules when you are on the track is never get in the car with a black man. Supposedly, he's either a cop or a pimp. I tried, but I couldn't turn him down; he was fine! He insisted that he wasn't a pimp or a cop, so I got in the car. We pulled up to a big, beautiful home with three cars in the drive way. I asked him who else lived there. He said he lived alone and those were his cars. I knew he was rich when I walked into the five bedroom home and saw how extravagant it was. I asked him where he worked and he told me he's a music producer. When we went into his bedroom, he sat me down and asked me why was I doing this. He told me that I could be anything I wanted to be; why choose prostitution? I avoided the question because I was too embarrassed and ashamed to give an answer. He asked if I would wash the make-up off my face so he can see my true beauty, and when I did, he kept complimenting me and caressing my face. He made me feel like a woman and not a prostitute. For once this was personal, not business. My *Pretty Woman* dreams were coming true. He's gorgeous, he's rich, and he likes me. He offered me a way out of the game. However, in my stupidity, I declined and chose to continue hustling. The truth is, I didn't see what he saw and I didn't think I deserved him. My dream came true for just one night only and then I woke up to my cold, hard reality.

My reality was disastrous. I was a sixteen-year old prostitute. I knew this life wasn't for me and the more I did it, the more I hated myself. I was ashamed and disappointment by my own actions. I was a high school dropout, getting drunk and hanging out with prostitutes and strippers, sleeping with men all day, then going home to a woman. My family was also disappointed in me. I tried to reach out to my dad and he would talk to me over the phone every once in a while, but he never wanted to see me. I didn't tell him what I was involved in. I just really needed him at that moment in my life, but he refused to be there. Many times I begged him to come and get me, but he said no again and again. I cried, yelled, screamed, and pleaded with him, but he wasn't moved. It had been four years since the last time we were together, and I didn't care about the past; I just wanted my daddy. I desperately needed him to wrap his arms around me and tell me he loved me, but it never happened.

I didn't know what else to do, so I turned to God once again and went to church to get encouraged. I never actually left the church no matter what was going on in my life, but after the mothers in the church turned their noses up at me, and the men slept with me for money, I no longer looked for help in the church. And if you can't get help in the church, where can you get it?

I never justified my lifestyle; I knew it was wrong. Every night I told god I was sorry for what I was doing. When the alcohol wore off I realized I had become something so degrading and foul, I just wanted out. I'm sure my neighbors listened as I screamed, "I WANNA DIE, GOD! I WANNA DIE!"

From Porn to the Pulpit

I lay on the floor and constantly asked Him to please take me, hoping that He would just kill me and put an end to this crap, but He never did. So I took matters into my own hands. Suicide knocked on my door again. I was at home alone and decided to take every pill in the medicine cabinet with hopes of going to sleep and never waking up. That didn't happen. Instead I woke up with a headache and an urge to vomit.

Accepting that death wasn't going to stop me from this life I made up my mind that this was it. I'm a prostitute, so I might as well be the best one out there. I changed my whole appearance, I dyed my hair blonde, I wore long French tip nails, my clothes became tighter and shorter and I wore green contacts. My look was inspired by the rapper *Lil Kim*. I completely lost myself. I got numerous tattoos and piercings all over my body. I made sure when you saw me you knew I was a prostitute. I didn't just do it; I became it.

I also viewed it as a way to get back at my father. I knew that I had become something that he hated, a lesbian and a prostitute. He had such high hopes for me to become a successful lawyer, but I chose prostitution instead of prosecution. I knew that once he discovered this, he really would never want to see me again. If he didn't want to be in my life for no reason, I was going to give him a real reason to not be there.

I managed to lose the one thing that I was yearning for, which was love. I eliminated every kind of emotion that was in me. I didn't give love and I didn't want it given to me. I figured without it no one could ever hurt me again. I put my feelings on the back burner and decided that money needed to be made.

Honey and I met up two or three times a week to go on dates together. She also had high paying clients who never paid anything less than a thousand dollars. Things went well until I found out that Honey had a secret that almost cost me my life.

I used to drop her off at an apartment in the Valley, but I never went in with her. One day I went to pick her up and I finally went inside. I sat on the couch waiting for her to get dressed. The front door opened and a tall, light skinned man walked in. He sat down and put his arm around me.

"Oh, she brought me a new one."

I yelled, "Get away from me!"

"Ooh, you feisty. I gotta tame you.

He pulled my hair and kissed me in the mouth. I slapped him and he grabbed me by my throat. Honey ran out the bathroom and said, "Tay don't hit her, she don't know!"

I snatched away from him and said, "What don't I know?"

"Queen, just wait for me outside, please."

I walked out pretending like I went to my car, but I stood at the door listening, and I heard Honey say, "I haven't told her yet, but I'm gonna' tell her tonight."

"Tay" started beating her immediately. He said, "You been hangin' with her long enough and she still hasn't chose me? Is she your pimp now?"

Trying to catch her breath, she said "No."

"You got two days. I want her here!"

I went to my car and a few minutes later, Honey came too. When she got into the car, her mouth was bleeding, her wig was twisted to the side, and her nails were broken. She lit her blunt and laid back in the seat.

I said, "Um, don't you think you need to explain yourself? What's going on?"

"Tay is my pimp. He knew I was getting money

Pimps & Prostitutes

with you and he wanted me to bring you back with me, so you can work for him too."

I was highly upset. I said, "So you didn't think I should've known that you have a pimp? You know what Honey I'm cool on you. I can't mess with you no more. You know I don't do pimps!"

She cried and said, "Queen, I'm so sorry! We can still get money together. He doesn't have to know."

I couldn't say no to her while she was crying, so I agreed to still do business with her behind Tay's back.

The following weekend we went to a super bowl party in Hollywood. The guy wanted a lot of dancers to attend and he paid in advance. The night went well and I made a couple hundred dollars dancing, while Honey made her money in the bedroom. When we left the party we stopped at a nearby gas station. I went in to pay, but while I was in there, I heard Honey screaming. I ran outside to see what was wrong with her. Tay was beating her up. He dragged her out of my car, kicking and punching her, and then he threw her into his car. When he saw me, he pulled out a gun and started shooting at me in the middle of the street. I ran but

From Porn to the Pulpit

he kept coming. He didn't stop until he ran out of bullets. I hid in someone's backyard for a few hours because I saw Tay driving back and forth looking for me. I guess he rather me be dead and not pay him, than to be alive and not pay him. I couldn't believe this man was really trying to kill me just because I didn't want to be his prostitute!

After Tay gave up on his search for me, I left the backyard and went to an after hour in L.A. I didn't want to go home fearing he would find me there, so I sat at the bar ordering drink after drink until I vomited and passed out on the bathroom floor. A stripper named, "Asia" came in there and saw me lying on the side of the toilet. She helped me up and told me to ease up on the liquor. She reached into her purse and said, "Here, I got something that won't make you throw up." She handed me a little bag of cocaine. Although I've tried marijuana and crystal meth with Natalie, I wasn't really into the drug thing. I just liked to get drunk. I guess that drunken spirit was passed down to me from my mother and father, but I had so much drama going on, I needed something stronger than Gin and juice. Asia put a line of cocaine on the sink and handed me a rolled up five dollar bill. She said, "Go ahead;

sniff it." When I did, it burned just as bad as the crystal meth. Asia laughed and said, "Give it a few minutes you'll be alright."

An hour passed and nothing happened. I didn't feel any different. I went to Asia and said, "Your drugs don't work. I don't feel anything."

"My bad, Queen. I thought it would do the job, but I got something else for you."

She handed me a yellow pill with a happy face on it. I swallowed it and she said, "I bet this will work!"

Chapter 7

Xstacy

I experimented with marijuana, cocaine, crystal meth and every kind of alcohol there is, but nothing could compare to Xstacy. The night Asia gave me that pill, something in me came alive. I was like a zombie that arose from the dead. It took a while for the pill to kick in, but when it did! After I took the pill I was a little nervous when my pupils dilated, I started sweating, and my heart was beating fast. I heard voices and I couldn't stop touching myself. I was so high that I couldn't walk, so I crawled over to Asia and said, "What did you give me?"

She looked at my condition and said, "Aw, man I

wasn't supposed to give you the whole pill. I should've broke it in half first. You alright?"

I smiled and said, "Got any more?"

I never heard about Xstacy before that night. I didn't even know what was in it. I later found out that it takes heroin, crack cocaine, meth, and whatever other drugs to make one little pill. Had I known that at first, maybe I wouldn't have taken it, but it was too late now. I met my match. My body instantly took to it and I had to have it. When I was high, it took me to another place. It gave me the satisfaction that no other drug had ever given me. In the beginning, I took Xstacy only twice a week, but before I knew it, I found myself craving it every day. The thing about X is that your high will only last for a few hours; then you sober up completely. I never wanted to be sober. So one pill a day turned into two, then three pills a day. One X pill can kill you, but I managed to get all the way up to four pills a day.

I had the "X Man" (drug dealer) on speed dial. I bought two hundred dollars worth of pills on a weekly basis. If the X Man ran out of supply, I became illogical. I couldn't function without it. I became extremely upset, sad, depressed, and bored.

Xstacy

I blamed the X Man for the way I was feeling, it was his fault because he didn't have the drugs. He just laughed and said, "Queen you're crazy." I went to the club one night, annoyed, because I didn't have any pills. I thought I could smoke marijuana, snort cocaine, and have a few drinks to make up for not having the X, but it didn't have the same effect. Luckily for me, almost all of the other strippers were addicted to alcohol or some kind of drug, so if I needed a fix, I knew where to get it. I hated asking people for stuff, but in this case I swallowed my pride. I had to have that pill. It became a priority and I did whatever I had to do to get it, even if it meant embarrassing myself.

I'd been dancing for quite some time at various clubs and parties, but the thought of dancing nude in front of strange men was definitely not an easy thing to do. That's where the drugs and alcohol came in. The alcohol would loosen me up and take the shyness away. It also helped me to cope with the wild aggressive men I had to deal with night after night. But when I took Xstacy, it not only loosened me up, it changed me. I walked differently, I talked differently, and I even danced differently. It brought out another side of me. The sober me was friendly, polite, and simple, but the high me was fierce, bold, and aggressive.

Although I was a stripper and an escort, I wasn't very sexual in my personal life. I preferred a relationship rather than just sex, but X changed all of that. I began wanting sex quite often, and I do mean often. My everyday routine consisted of X, sex, and money.

I would come up with schemes on how to get as many pills as possible. My next plot was to hook up with the X Man. He already had a crush on me and he wasn't bad looking, so I put my plan into action. I called and asked him if I could meet him somewhere. He said, "Meet me in Watts, at the spot." I put on my shortest dress and highest heels, a pound of make-up, and headed to Watts to see if my plan would work. When I got there, the door was unlocked. I didn't say anything; I just walked in and seduced him. After we had sex I told him a bunch of stories about how much I wanted to be with him, he should be my man, and a whole bunch of other fibs. I was lying through my teeth, but he believed it. I looked on the table and saw at least a hundred pills in a bag. I inquired about them and he told me he was going to sell them. I suggested that he give them to me. He looked at me with hesitation, but remembering our little episode, he handed me the whole bag. I stayed a few extra minutes and then I left on cloud nine.

Sadly, I went through a hundred pills in three weeks. I called the X Man and told him I needed more, he yelled and asked where did all the pills go? I didn't want to sound like an addict, even though I was one, so I told him one of the strippers went into my bag and took them. He believed me, offered to buy me a lock, and give me some more pills. I met him in Watts at the spot again, but this time it wasn't as many pills as before. It was about forty which was fine because it was more than what I had.

Xstacy took over my life. With the money I was making at the club and with my clients, I should've had a lot more material things, but all the money went to my drug habit. I would rather buy X than pay my bills or go shopping with my girls. Violet couldn't understand where all the money was going. She had no idea that I was spending it on drugs.

Time passed and frightening things started happening to my health. I consumed so many drugs that I began having seizures. I was at a private party one night, and while I was dancing I passed out. I assumed that I was overly intoxicated. When I opened my eyes, there were four men standing over me. I don't know what they did to me, but I woke up totally naked. Other times, I woke up in the middle of the night in a cold sweat or high fever. Violet would come home to find me laid out, seizing, on the living room floor. These episodes happened every other week. I tried to ignore all of this until I woke up in the hospital with a fever of one hundred and three. At first the doctors didn't understand why this was happening until they did multiple tests. I had a dangerous amount of drugs in my system which was causing the seizures. My consumption of X had gotten so bad that the D.M.V suspended my driver's license because, being subject to unpredictable seizures, I was legally unable to operate a vehicle. The doctor told me that if I continued using drugs there was no doubt that I would eventually die. With the warning I received, I unfortunately continued on with my heavy drug use. No matter what happened to me I refused to be sober.

Most people with common sense would have

Xstacy

stopped using Xstacy or any other drugs right away, but I didn't. Even though it was killing me I couldn't stop. It helped me to escape my reality. It took the pain away (for the moment.) For instance, I couldn't think about Samaja without crying uncontrollably, even after all this time. In fact, his birthday and Mother's Day were the most dreadful events for me to endure. So I took a pill. I couldn't think about my dad without becoming enraged, so I took a pill. A few of my stripper friends were murdered and instead of me attending funerals, I took a pill. It helped me to prostitute myself because I could never do it in a sober state of mind. I wanted to give up this life, but I couldn't. No matter what I went through, no matter how bad it got, I couldn't stop. I was addicted.

Chapter 8

The Addiction

My hunger for money grew stronger. The more money I made the more I wanted. I was at a point where I would have done absolutely anything for it. In fact, my craving for Xstacy was nothing compared to my craving for money. I was never satisfied; too much was never enough. I wanted more and I did a whole lot to get it.

I started dancing at two clubs. I went to a strip club in the Valley for the day shift and then I went to another club in Hawthorne for the night shift. When the clubs were closed I would go to an after hour, and when that was over I went to see some my clients. I stayed up for two or three days at a time because the Xstacy and cocaine wouldn't allow me to sleep, so I stayed up all night chasing money. I was making at least four thousand dollars a week between dancing and my clients, but that wasn't enough, especially since I had an expensive drug habit to feed. In order for me to get more I had to do more.

No matter how miserable my life was at that time, as long as I had money in my pocket it didn't matter. I cared more about the money than I did myself. That's what made it easy for me to continue with this horrible lifestyle. Money was my motivation. I wanted more and more and I got it.

One night, while I was dancing at the club in Hawthorne, a couple of porn stars came in named, "Fire" and "Uniya." I knew exactly who they were. I saw them in a few movies I owned. I approached Fire to say hello and to let her know that I've seen some of her work, but the conversation went a different way. She asked me if I was interested in doing porn movies. I quickly responded and said, "Absolutely not!"

She laughed and asked, "Why not? You like money don't you? It's one thing to watch porn, but it's another thing to actually do it. Indeed, I was a

The Addiction

known stripper and prostitute, but porn was taking it a little too far, and I wasn't interested in that.

Fire said, "You should do it; if you think you're making money now, you ain't seen nothin' yet. You'll be doing the same thing you're doing now; the only difference is you'll be in front of a camera." She handed me her card and said, "Call me."

All night I kept looking at that card wondering if I should call her. I tried to imagine myself having sex in front of a camera or with other people being around. I even thought about the money that could be made in that industry. When the drugs and alcohol wore off I came to my senses and decided not to go through with it, but the girls and I became good friends. I didn't need porn; I was balling already. I was dancing at two clubs, I had my high paying clients on the side, and I hooked up with a Jamaican drug dealer who put me on his team.

His name was "Lion." I met him at a Jamaican night club in Hollywood. He was big time. He had homes in New York, Miami, Jamaica, and when he was in L.A. he stayed in five star hotels. He wasn't attractive by any means, but what caught my attention was the black Bentley he was driving. All that meant to me was that he had money and I wanted it! So, I stood in front of him making sure he noticed me, and he did. He walked over to me and said, "I want you." I flirted back and we exchanged numbers. That night he called and asked me to meet him at his hotel room.

I said, "I only go to hotel rooms if its money there."

"Come now!"

I pulled up to the Beverly Hills Hilton where he was staying. I went to his room and he was sitting on the bed smoking weed.

I said, "I don't think you can smoke in here."

He laughed and said, "I'm Lion. I do what I want."

He asked me a lot of questions to get an understanding of who I was. I believe he just wanted to make sure I wasn't an undercover cop. He must've felt comfortable with me because he went to the closet and pulled out three big suitcases full of weed, cocaine, and X pills. He asked me to bag them up for him. He saw the expression on my face and said, "Don't worry. I will pay you."

As I bagged the drugs up for him, he came behind me and said, "I want you on my team."

We slept together that night and when we

The Addiction

finished Lion got up and walked over to the closet a second time. He opened another suitcase, but this one had a large amount of money in it. He pulled out two thousand dollars and handed it to me. I was surprised. I didn't expect him to give me that much. He saw the confusion on my face and said, "What? You don't want the money?"

We laughed and shortly after that I left, but I made it my duty to keep in contact with him. He traveled most of the time, but we saw each other often. Every time he was in L.A. he called me. Things were good, and they got even better.

A few months later, Lion and I were still seeing each other. One night he called and asked me to come to his hotel room to talk. When I got there he had six suitcases on the bed.

He said, "You been my girl for a while now and I trust you a little. I want you to do a job for me." I was extremely nervous, I thought he was going to ask me to kill somebody; he looked so serious.

He continued and said, "All I want you to do is take these suitcases to my partner. He'll be at your club once a week and I'll pay you every time."

Without delay I said, "Okay! I'll do it."

He laughed and said, "That was fast. You can

start tonight."

I was paid well! Lion gave me large amounts of money every time I saw him. I did the drop offs once a week, I sold drugs to the girls at the club. I was dancing and escorting. I knew that I would face hard jail time if I ever got caught with the drugs, but I took that risk. I was making about eight thousand dollars a week, if not more. I had so much money and I was never going to stop. I was seventeen years old making more money in a month than most adults make in a year. I was addicted to my new lifestyle. Lion made all my dreams come true and I stopped making him pay to be with me. After all, it was because of him that I had so much money. Life was good. I had money, I had jewelry, I had drugs, and I partied like a Rock Star every night of the week.

All that came to an unexpected end when Lion got into trouble. He was deported back to Jamaica and my money stopped. I couldn't make moves without him. I mean, don't get me wrong, I had money before him, but it didn't compare to the money I made with him. I had to come up with another plan; fast.

Chapter 9

Porn

I was at home thinking about how I was going to support myself now that Lion was in jail. I had an apartment, a car, and bills that needed to be paid. I didn't want to stress myself out at that time, so I ignored it. To keep my mind occupied, I started cleaning up my apartment one day and came across the card that Fire, the porn star, gave me. As I looked at the card, I knew automatically that I didn't want to do porn; but what other option did I have? I sure wasn't about to get a job. No job could ever come close to giving me the kind of money that I was making, and I wasn't about to wait two

From Porn to the Pulpit

weeks for a check that I could get in one day. Who was going to hire me, anyway? I'm seventeen years old with little work experience and no high school diploma. McDonald's wouldn't even hire me. So I had to do what I had to do, whether I liked it or not.

It was strange because the exact moment the thought entered my head "Michelle" called and asked me to carpool with her to the Valley. Michelle was a lesbian girl that I met in the gay click a few years back and she recently started doing porn. I was confused when she started doing porn because she was so "anti-man." However, when money is involved, you'd be surprised what people will do. I was in a relationship myself, but I was still prostituting and stripping, so I definitely understood where she was coming from. As soon as she arrived at my place, we left and headed to the Valley; also known as the "Porn Capital."

On the way there, Michelle talked about how excited she was about the movie she made and how she couldn't wait to do more. She told me how great her experience was, and she encouraged me to join the industry as well. We arrived at a mansion, and we were barely inside when I heard a lot of noises; moaning and screaming to be exact. I

Porn

peeked around the corner and saw a lot of naked people having sex. They had no shame. They looked so comfortable, like they were in the privacy of their own bedrooms. There was a camera man, a director, and at least ten people doing an orgy scene. I stood there in awe as a porno was being filmed right in front of my face. I had porn friends who told me about the things that went on, but I never went on set with any of them. Seeing this for the first time was definitely mind blowing.

Michelle pulled me away from the room where the porn stars were, and introduced me to her agent, a female named "Robbie." She was extremely funny and right away Robbie took an interest in me. She asked if I'd ever done porn before. Michelle answered before me and said, "Nope, she's fresh fish."

Robbie smiled and said, "I can get a lot of work for you. Are you ready?"

I wanted to say NO!!! But I just grinned and said, "Yeah, I'm ready."

Immediately, she called over a porn director from West Coast Productions and introduced me to him. He told me to follow him into one of the bedrooms. When I entered the room, he shut the door behind him and said, "Take your clothes off. Let me see what you got."

I was extremely apprehensive which is why I always had to be intoxicated when situations like this would occur. Unfortunately, I was sober and very uncomfortable with taking my clothes off in front of this porn man. In a very weird way, he examined my body with his eyes and then he asked for my age. I lied and said I was eighteen. I knew they would go crazy if they knew I was only seventeen, and technically, a senior in high school.

"Eighteen?" he said arrogantly. "Don't you know this industry is for grown folks?"

I smiled sarcastically and he said, "I'll talk to Robbie about you."

I hung around the mansion and took pictures with the famous porn stars, until it was time to go. Robbie gave me her card and told me to call her a.s.a.p. When I got home I thought long and hard about my next move.

Still not knowing what to do, I put the thought on the back burner because my eighteenth birthday was coming up and my girlfriend Violet wanted to take me to Hawaii. We spent a week in Hawaii and when we came back, I headed to the club where I

Porn

danced. Not long after I arrived, I received a phone call from Michelle saying that a stripper I danced with beat her up. My loyalty quickly kicked in and I was ready to handle the situation for my so-called friend. That next night I was supposed to be off, but I headed to the club to confront the stripper that jumped Michelle, but I wasn't alone. I took my gun with me. I stepped to the girl in the dressing room, pulled my gun out, and scared her into believing that I was going to shoot her for what she did to Michelle. Out of fear the girl went to the manager and snitched on me. He came up to me and asked if I had a gun, of course I lied and said no. He went through my bag and found the gun. He fired me from the club that same night. He was happy to do it too, because unlike the other strippers, I wouldn't sleep with him.

Now what was I going to do? I couldn't sell drugs anymore because Lion was gone, I couldn't strip because I got fired, so now what? Bills were piling up, my drug habit needed attention, and I was close to broke. It all happened overnight. I went from having everything to almost being evicted from my apartment.

I had to do it. In March of 2007, four days after

my eighteenth birthday, I called Robbie and told her I was ready. She gave me the address to A.I.M, the S.T.D. testing center for adult entertainers. Being in porn you have to get tested every twenty-eight days (as if that mattered; people in the industry still became infected with various diseases). When I got to the testing center, I took a urine and blood test. The next day my results came back negative and I was ready to work. Robbie called me and said, "I got your test results and everything is good. I have a boy/girl scene for you to do tomorrow." I wasn't expecting it to happen so fast. I really wasn't expecting it to happen at all, but it did.

I just had to make sure my family would never find out about it. My mother and I had just started getting along again. I couldn't ruin it by telling her I was doing porn. She knew I was stripping and she wasn't happy with that at all, but me doing porn would devastate her, and especially my grandparents. I also had to come up with a really good lie to tell Violet. I knew she wasn't going to stay with me if she knew that I was doing porn or anything that included men. After giving it a lot of thought I told Violet that I was only going to do

Porn

girl/girl scenes, hoping she would never find out that I was engaging in sex scenes with men too (on and off camera.) She was upset and said no at first, but it was my money that supported her too, so she really didn't have a choice.

The time had now come for me to go to "work." I met Robbie at another mansion in the Valley. She greeted me and told me to, "Go and sit in the chair for hair and make-up." I had knots in my stomach. I was beyond nervous. I knew I didn't want to be there, but it was too late for me to leave and my addiction for money wouldn't allow me to.

A few minutes later a male porn star named "Nate" showed up and that man was fine! I started to loosen up very quickly when I saw him. (I was weak when it came to good looking men.) He knew it was my first scene, so he was really nice and tried to make me feel comfortable (at first.)

Unfortunately, I wasn't that comfortable because I was still sober. There was no way that I could do the scene in a sober state, so I went to my "goody bag." I popped an X pill and drunk a shot of Tequila. Once I got high, it wasn't that bad. I had a good looking brother that I was about to work with, I'm about to get paid, and the celebrity treatment with everyone catering to me was just what I needed. Yep, I was ready (or so I thought.)

The photographer took solo pictures of me first, then of Nate and I took pictures together. After that, it was time to start the scene. I thought I was numb from the drugs I'd taken earlier, but his penis was so large and I felt every bit of it. It was not as I imagined. Now, don't get me wrong; I've had lots of sex as a prostitute, but those men weren't large at all. I later found out that a man has to be at least nine inches in order to do porn. Nate was around eleven or twelve inches. (Ouch!) I had never been with a man that size, and didn't want to be. We started off slowly, then we sped things up toward the middle, but at end it was very fast and rough. And did I mention painful? Since it was my first scene, Nate called himself, "breaking me in." Anytime a male porn star gets a girl on her first scene, he must prove a point. Leaving himself memorable, which means he shows no mercy to the female performer.

Although we were both tested, I was still a little uneasy about us not using a condom and that made it even worse. Right before I decided to do porn, someone in the industry got infected with H.I.V and the industry was forced to shut down for a

Porn

while (and that wasn't the first time.) The whole time Nate and I were "performing" I thought about that.

Then, the director instructed us to change positions after a certain amount of time and to talk dirty to each other. He wanted me to seductively look into the camera, but I had a hard time doing that because I was in an awkward situation, plus I was in pain. The scene lasted about forty-five minutes. I screamed from beginning to end and not because of pleasure. It felt like he was ripping me apart and this was just movie number one.

When I got home I avoided Violet and headed straight to the bathroom. I soaked in the tub for hours with tears in my eyes because the pain was so unbearable. My conscience started to kick in and I asked myself, "Has it really come down to this? You just did a porno!" All these thoughts came through my mind concerning my relationship with Violet, my family, diseases, and pregnancy. I could have made a decision to stop at that moment, but I had no determination to stop. I had no self-worth and I didn't think that I could ever do anything else. After that the scenes started coming in back to back, giving my body no time to heal. I knew porn was not going to be something enjoyable, but I had to get the money.

Throughout all of this I was still in church hoping and praying that someone in the church would see my pain and just come up to me and tell me that I'm better than this, but it never happened. The mothers in the church rejected me as if I was an alien or something. They treated me worse than I treated myself. I could feel their stares and hear their whispers about me. The men in the church preyed on me instead of prayed for me. In fact, they became my biggest clients. All I wanted someone to do was help me get out of this. Instead, they shut me out, which only fueled my fire even more. So I left church, popped an X pill, and prepared myself to do more porn.

A few weeks later I was already on movie number twenty, which happened to be a girl/girl scene. I befriended "Kacey," a porn star who was in the business for a year. At first she seemed real boogie and stuck up like most of the other women in the industry, but when I got to know her she was really nice. We started hanging out every day and I really liked her because of the lifestyle she introduced me to.

Porn

Kacey had celebrity clientele. She was V.I.P at every club, she attended every celebrity event she could get to, and I was right there with her. Being in porn, you have easy access to mainstream celebrities. I was amazed when I found out that many celebrities are big fans of pornography. They attend many porn functions and become very excited when in the presence of the porn star of their choice.

Being with Kacey not only enhanced my lifestyle, but it changed my attitude as well. Although I was a stripper and adult entertainer, I was still very humble and down to earth. I had no problem going to hang out in the "hood." I didn't care about being with celebrities, or obtaining V.I.P. status. None of that meant anything to me until I got with her. I thought I was "somebody" because now I had celebrities contacting me and paying to sleep with me. Rappers, athletes, comedians, actors; you name it. The same people I watched on television and listened to on the radio were in my bed.

I stopped hanging with the people who didn't have the kind of money I had, or more. I started spending outrageous amounts of money on clothes and bags. My image was also starting to change. I was considering getting breast implants to enhance my look. Every man that I dealt with had to be rich or famous. I wouldn't talk to "regular people" that had "regular money." I became more materialistic. I had to have the best and I turned into a monster. Kacey would always remind me that we were celebrities too. We were in movies and in magazines, we had fans just like the football players and rappers, and I started to believe that lie. I believed that I was really a celebrity, but in reality I was just a prostitute working on movie number thirty. I tried to live an upscale lifestyle, I bought a brand new 2008 truck, I moved to the Valley, and went to clubs where only mainstream celebrities and porn stars attended. I became unapproachable because I was so cocky and conceited. We had it going on for a while, but that didn't last very long.

Kacey and I would often fall out. I felt she was senseless when it came to getting money. I guess she thought traveling with rappers and athletes, expensive dinners, and the V.I.P. treatment at the club was enough for her to spread eagle. I wasn't playing that. I wanted the money. I didn't care who you were; my body was a business. It agitated me when she would go on trips for days with these

Porn

men and come back empty handed. I tried to explain to her numerous times that she was a prostitute and prostitutes get paid. She would reply by saying, "I'm not a hoe, I'm a porn star! There's a difference! Hoes don't get to travel with rappers and basketball players, but porn stars do. A prostitute stands on the corner and they don't have celebrity contacts!" Sadly, so many of the women in the industry believed that same lie, but I didn't care what they said. I knew what we were.

We continued back and forth, but decided to keep doing our own thing. I didn't care how famous they were. If they wanted me they had to pay. After all, I was a celebrity too. Right? Kacey and I started to grow apart rapidly. I explained to her numerous times how to get money from these men, but it seemed as if she was scared of asking, fearing that if she asked they would exclude her. I guess just being a part of their celebrity circle and having private time with them was good enough for her to drop it like it's hot. I felt like she was giving me a bad name. Since she was known to give you a good time for free they expected me to do the same, and that wasn't happening. I wanted to be around go-getters; women who had a passion for money like I did. Kacey and I stopped talking and we actually became enemies. I was happy with one thing she did. She introduced me to a new life. I was addicted to the money, fame, and celebrity men. I had no plans on giving it up.

I was in the industry for less than a year and already making a name for myself. People recognized who I was. I couldn't walk down the street without a guy yelling out my name. I was really flabbergasted when women paid to come and see me perform. I was meeting more and more celebrities, I was invited to B.E.T parties and Grammy parties, clubs were paying me to fly out and dance. I was signing autographs and traveling. It was all good for a second, but every bad thing comes to an end.

After the fascination of being in the porn industry was over, reality finally kicked in. I started noticing things that weren't right. Caucasian porn stars make far more money than African-American porn stars. The industry has the nerve to be prejudice.

The so-called agents booked girls and lied to them about how much money the scene actually paid. For example, if the scene paid a thousand dollars, the agent struck a deal with the director

Porn

and paid the girl only four or five hundred dollars of her own money. A majority of the agents were doing this; cheating girls and guys out of their money. If you ask me, that's being a pimp, not an agent. I felt so sorry for some of the guys and girls, but then again, I wondered why they didn't check into this for themselves. The male agents also force the new girls to sleep with them first, claiming they had to see if they were good enough for the scenes, and the new girls fell for it because they didn't know any better. As if that weren't bad enough, things got a little more interesting.

A certain female porn star that had been in the industry for a while performed such excessive anal intercourse that a piece of muscle from her anus fell out on set, while filming.

Other females damaged their reproductive systems to such an extent that they were left unable to have children. One male porn star broke the muscle in his penis because he was having abnormal and outrageously rough sex on set. I also found out that one veteran, male porn star was a devil worshipper. Both male and female porn stars were committing suicide.

To make sure they were able to perform, the male

porn stars were pumped with limitless Viagra. A lot of the female porn stars have pimps and are forced to do porn. Everybody was on drugs (including me), from marijuana to heroine. No one was ever sober. Most of the men in the industry are homosexuals. Even some of the straight ones go gay-for-pay. Most porn stars are forced to do alarmingly more, hardcore scenes in order to continue in the business.

A lot of porn stars were known to go overseas and do bestiality porn (sex with animals). Shortly after that, numerous porn stars turned up with diseases; Herpes to be exact. The industry allows one to work as long as you're not having an outbreak. They want them to believe that they cannot pass a disease if the sores are not visible. I knew Chlamydia and Gonorrhea were common in the industry because I've seen it for myself. A female porn star caught Gonorrhea in her eye. I've heard stories of people catching it in their anuses and throats. I knew one guy in particular who always had one S.T.D or another, and nobody wanted to work with him. When they booked me to do a scene with him, I was highly upset and the hypocrisy kicked in. I prayed to God and begged

Porn

Him not to let me catch a disease. Thankfully, I never did. Although I never caught a disease in the industry I did have the scare of my life.

We were at the 2008 AVN Awards in Las Vegas. (Porn Convention) After the award show everyone in the industry would get drunk and high and have sex with whomever they wanted, so stupidly, I engaged in this activity as well. With a few drinks and a lot of drugs, a young lady and I decided to have a rendezvous with two male porn stars at the Venetian Hotel. When we finished, a third guy walked into the room. I had the biggest crush on him while I was in the industry and badly wanted to work with him, but for some reason it never happened. When he walked into the hotel room this was my opportunity to finally sleep with him. But then something strange happened. A sudden heaviness came over me and I was too tired to do anything, so the girl who was there with me had sex with him instead.

When the AVN was over, she and I left together and started escorting. We went to a hotel in Pasadena to work, but weren't feeling so well. Both of us had similar symptoms, but she found a huge bump on her vagina which scared the crap out of both of us, so we decided to make a doctor's appointment. Her appointment was Monday and mine was Wednesday. When Monday afternoon came I got a phone call from her. She was crying and said that she had Herpes!

I lost my breath and dropped the phone. My body collapsed to the floor. I screamed and cried for hours. I just knew that I had it too! We had sex with the same people! I begged and pleaded with God, asking Him to not let me have this disease. For the next two days I didn't eat or sleep. I just prayed, lying to the Lord, telling Him that if I didn't have Herpes, I would stop doing porn. Just please don't let me have that disease!

I went to the doctor's office on Wednesday morning and asked my doctor to test me for EVERYTHING! I told her about the dumb decision I made in Vegas and to see if I had Herpes. She told me, "When you have Herpes you will know it because it's a visible disease." She tested me and said that I definitely didn't have Herpes or any other diseases. I thought that this was impossible because we were with the same people. Then, I suddenly remembered that I didn't have sex with the guy I really liked, but my friend did. He was the

Porn

one who gave her the Herpes.

I didn't know it then, but God had His hand on me even in my wickedness. I was so careless with my life and health and He still protected me, even when I didn't protect myself. (Luke 6:35: For He is kind to the unthankful and evil.){ NKJV}

Although He saved me yet again, I went back on my word. I stopped doing porn for about two months and attended church more often bringing other porn stars with me. In my mind I was thanking Him for protecting me, hoping I would really make a change. I truly wanted to be done with the industry, so I decided to dance only, but this was unendurable for me. The money wasn't the same. My addiction for the lifestyle started to rise up again and I couldn't ignore it anymore. I battled with myself about going back to the industry. I promised God that I wouldn't go back if He made sure I didn't have any diseases. I felt bad because He kept His word and I didn't. Unfortunately, at that time money and drugs were my god. I needed it more than anything else. I knew it was wrong, but I tried to negotiate with Him. I said I wouldn't do boy/girl movies anymore; I would only do girl/girl movies to avoid catching a disease (as if that was any better.) I did lesbian movies for a few weeks, but there's not much money in that genre. Eventually, I went back to doing scenes with men.

Around this time, the scenes were getting more and more difficult. I became involved in more than I could handle. In the beginning, I was certain that I would only do "regular scenes" but that soon changed. When I entered the industry I performed in solo, boy/girl, and girl/girl scenes, which were considered "regular." As time went on, I began doing orgies and other abominable things. The rule is, the more you do, the more money you get. My first orgy scene was awful. I was on set for fourteen hours. My body shut down after that night. It felt like I let twelve other people torture me. I hated doing orgies. I hated doing porn, period; but I loved the lifestyle and I paid a big price for it.

Things took a turn for the worse after that. My body started going through so many changes. My menstrual cycle became irregular. I went months without having a period and I wasn't pregnant. There would be times when I couldn't get out of bed because I was in so much pain from doing a scene. I literally crawled around on the floor. The guys in that industry were so rough and careless. I

Porn

doubt that they actually considered us to be human beings. We were just a piece of meat to them. My weight also went up and down.

There were days when I wouldn't eat at all and other days I ate excessively. I was in and out of the hospital as my seizures got worse from the excessive consumption of so many drugs, and yet I increased my drug use. It was no longer just Xstacy and cocaine, it was now all of that, crystal meth and heroine. My doctor was tired of seeing me. I was so paranoid about catching diseases that I made appointments for S.T.D checks three times a month. Then, I became psychotic because of all the soul ties and spirits that came along from sleeping with a multitude of people. I literally went crazy. One minute I was fine, the next, I was sitting in a corner rocking back and forth, screaming, crying, and cursing for no reason. I was prescribed Prozac because the psychiatrist said I was Bipolar (like my daddy.)

The truth is I was losing my mind because I really didn't want to do porn. I didn't want to prostitute myself. I didn't want to do any of it anymore, but I felt I had to stay in it, even though it was tearing me apart; both internally and

From Porn to the Pulpit

externally. I hated my life and took my anger out on women, beating them the same way men beat me. (After three years,) Violet left me because she finally found out that I was having sex with men the whole time we were together. At that time, I became very suicidal all over again. I desperately wanted to die. I lay in my bed and asked God to end my life. I didn't want to live like this anymore, but I couldn't stop. It had a hold on me. The only thing that could stop me was death.

People glorify pornography like it's so great and that's what the industry wants you to believe, but it's absolutely horrifying. If it's so great, why do so many porn stars commit suicide? If it's so great, why did we all have to be intoxicated to do a scene? When I went to the Adult Expos and Porn Conventions, men and women jumped for joy when they saw me. I smiled and sashayed around, participating in the deception, but I always wondered if they would still like me if they knew that this industry made me sick to my stomach.

Would they still like me if they knew I was really a lesbian and that I hated men? Would they still like me if they knew I cried every time I had to perform?

Porn

I figured they liked me so much because I satisfied their perverted imaginations. I fulfilled their lustful thoughts. It was my fault, but I never liked having pity parties for myself. I had to stay focused on hustling and faking like everything was alright, and as always, I brushed it under the rug and kept going on with my wretched life.

Just when I thought things couldn't get any worse, I ran into Kye while I was out shopping. For years I carried so much hatred towards him because of what he did to me and my son. I always thought that if I ever saw him again I would probably kill him, but that didn't happen. His charm overwhelmed me. He apologized continually for what he did when I was pregnant with Samaja. I took things slowly with him, but I eventually ended up back in his bed.

When I was with him he made me feel like a true drug addict. Every time we were together we did drugs for hours. He started abusing me again and forcing me to have sex with him. I stayed with him because I felt we had a connection because of our son, and I was so used to being abused it didn't even matter at that point. When Kye found out that I was doing porn, his pimping skills kicked in and he wanted me to work for him. Of course, I declined and he accepted that.

We decided to go our separate ways until I found out I was pregnant. When I told him, history had repeated itself. He denied that he was the father yet again, but this time he had reason to. After all, I was doing porn. I questioned who the father was myself, but I truly believed the baby was Kye's. What are the odds of me not getting pregnant for five years then all of sudden he comes back into my life and *Voila!* I'm pregnant again. I wasn't 100% sure that the baby was his because I was doing scenes and sleeping with him at the same time.

The male porn stars are not supposed to ejaculate inside the girls, but they do it, anyway. It was a definite possibility that it happened to me because it happened to the other girls all the time. I carried the baby for about twelve weeks, but I miscarried. I wasn't in a position to have a baby at that time of my life, anyway; especially not by Kye. What type of role model would we be to the child? I was a porn star and he was a pimp. It was shameful when I saw the other porn stars bringing their children to the set or to AIM. I just couldn't do that to my child.

Porn

I was in the industry for almost two years and the scenes were slowing down because directors wanted me to do anal scenes. For some reason anal was the new hot thing at that time. I always told myself that I would never do that, whether personally or professionally. That was one thing nobody could have; not to mention, it was a painful experience (so I've been told.) The girl whose muscle fell out of her anus was convincing enough for me never want to do it.

Altogether I was in about fifty movies, it could have been more, but I traveled a lot to dance and escort. When my fans questioned me about making more movies, I responded by telling them that, "I wasn't just a porn star, I was a dancer too, and I enjoyed dancing much more." In reality, I didn't like to dance either, but that was my way to escape the porn life and still make money. My agent, Robbie, used to call and say, "I have a scene for you..." but I was out of town. I called her back pretending like I was upset that I "missed out" on the movie. In actuality, I was relieved that I was gone and didn't have to do it.

I also thought that I had formed friendships with the other females in the industry but once again, that was not the case. All my life I desired to have a true friend; someone that wasn't going to talk about me behind my back, be jealous of me, or sleep with my boyfriend. For some strange reason I thought I would find that in these lovely porn stars. I befriended a lot of them because we would do scenes together, go to parties, and get money escorting, but drama always followed. They thought I was crazy too since I talked about God in most of our conversations, and encouraged them to go to church with me. I seemed very hypocritical and odd to them because they couldn't understand how I was doing porn, but loved church so much.

   I was over the whole porn click and decided that hanging with other women would just slow me down anyway. I got tired of the gossiping, the hating, and all the rest of the drama that comes with porn stars and strippers. I've been doing this long enough, so I decided to roll by myself, but that wasn't such a good idea.

Chapter 10

Please Don't Kill Me

Getting money on my own started off real good. I didn't have to split the money with the other girls or deal with any extra drama. I went to after hours, clubs, bachelor parties, porn sets, and even other states and countries by myself. Someone told me that I should hire a bodyguard, but I didn't think I needed one and I didn't want to pay for one.

It was a club in Hawthorne that I often went to and the same men would be there most of the time. One nerdy guy in particular would always be there. He was black, slim, tall, and he wore glasses. He stayed to himself; he was a little weird and extremely quiet. He was strange because after he'd tip me on stage, I would go over to thank him and he would walk away from me. I didn't pay it much attention; I just assumed he was shy.

I moved back to Hawthorne to dance, but I spent most of my time doing porn and escorting. I never ran into Valley people when I was in Hawthorne and vice versa, so it was odd when I started seeing this man in the Valley. He was at the grocery store, the cleaners, and the mall while I was there. I assumed it was just a coincidence. I started seeing his Lexus by my apartment. I thought that maybe he knew someone in the area. I didn't realize he was stalking me!

One night after leaving the club, I was on my way home and I got paranoid. I ignored it, thinking it was just the drugs I'd taken earlier. When I got home I was about to take a shower, but I left my bag in my car. When I went outside to get it, there was a long stem rose on my windshield. I picked it up, got my bag and walked back to my place. When I got to the door it was another rose which was not there when I first walked out. It was a lot of guys that lived in my apartment building, so I assumed it was one of them who put it there. After I got out of the shower I noticed someone walking back and forth by my bedroom window. I looked through the blinds, but I didn't see anyone. I was about to lay down when I heard someone trying to open my front door. I got up and looked out the peep hole and I saw him. The weirdo from the club was trying to break into my apartment. I ran to my bedroom to get my gun, but when I went back to the front door he was gone. I looked out of the window and saw him running to his car. The surprising thing was that I was more angry than afraid. I wondered what he planned to do to me if he had gotten in.

A few months later I went to a swinger's party in Chatsworth to dance. I met an Armenian man there who offered me money for sex. He didn't want to do it at the party he wanted to go to a hotel and I agreed. On the way to the hotel he started acting different. He wasn't as friendly as he was when we were at the party. He started beating the steering wheel and cursing for absolutely no reason. He passed a few hotels and started driving further away from the Chatsworth going towards Hollywood. I told him we were going too far and to go back to one of the hotels he passed by. He looked at me and got real quiet. He exited the freeway and drove into the Hollywood Hills. It was after midnight and pitch black outside. We were so far out that even if I screamed no one would hear me.

He finally stopped the car and I said, "I'm not feeling this I'm not doing nothing with you. I'm ready to go!"

He sniffed a line of cocaine and said, "You're not going anywhere."

I started cursing at him, he gave me an evil look and got out of the car and walked to the trunk. He pulled out a machete and got back into the car. It was a numbness that came over me. I couldn't scream, I couldn't run or move. It seemed unreal. All I could do was pray to God for protection, hoping that this man was not going to chop me in half. He put seven hundred dollars on the dashboard and said, "There's your money, now give me what I want." He snatched the condom out of my hand and put it on. I performed sexual acts on him with a machete to my throat. When it was over he told me to have a good day and to get out. I took a taxi back to the Valley to get my car, never once did I cry. I was relieved that I was alive and

Please Don't Kill Me

after all of that he still paid me.

The next week I went to a bar on Sunset and I met three Middle Eastern men. We were all drinking and having a good time, but I was there to work. One of them invited me back to his place and I asked him how much money did he have? He seemed caught off guard, but excited. He said, "Well since it's like that how about all three of us?"

"As long as all three of y'all have money."

We agreed to go back to their place and not thinking very well I left my car at the bar and rode with them. Everything went as planned until they turned into an alley. They started speaking in their language and the guy that was sitting in the back seat with me looked scared and nervous. When I saw his reaction it made me nervous. The driver got out of the car and got into the back seat with me. He handed me four hundred dollars and I told him that wasn't enough. He looked at me with a devious look and said, "Make it enough." Meanwhile, the other two were outside of the car arguing. I started having sex in the back seat of the Benz with the driver while watching the other two. The third guy that was nervous walked away and the passenger got back into the car. I knew something bad was about to happen. The passenger pulled a gun out of the glove compartment and asked me did I want to die. For a second, a part of me wanted to say yes. I figured if he killed me I wouldn't have to deal with this crap anymore. Then again I wanted more money, so I told him, "No, I don't want to die."

He got in the back seat and forced himself on me. The driver made fun of him because he only lasted for two minutes. Being embarrassed, he pointed the gun at me and threw me out of the car. I believe he was going to shoot me, but he didn't know how to cock the gun back. The third guy who didn't want to be a part of it looked at me with tears in his eyes and whispered, "I'm sorry." The sad thing about it is I think he had more compassion for me than I had for myself. When I went home, I was very upset, not because I got raped and almost killed, but because I didn't get all of the money I asked for. I figured if they were going to do me like that they could at least pay me for it. My addiction was more important than my own life.

I went back to the Valley which was infested with pimps. Every time I looked around they were right there ready to recruit more girls. I knew this was part of the game, but I had no clue of the extent that they were willing to go. When they saw me they knew I would never work for them. I was a "renegade." (A prostitute with no pimp.) I wouldn't risk losing my life, going to jail, and having sex all day just to give my money away. So they would try to run me over with their cars, throw me in their trunks, or beat me. One pimp was so obsessed he started following me. He even jumped out of the bushes and chased me into ongoing traffic. I almost got hit by a truck. I had to prepare myself for this every time I was in the company of pimps which was almost every day.

A few days after that I got a phone call from a stripper I danced with. She told me to be careful because our friend "Kayla's" body was just found. Kayla was a stripper, not a prostitute. She had two small daughters that she was taking care of by herself. She needed the extra money, so when she was approached by a man who wanted to pay her for sex she went for it. Her first time prostituting was also her last time because the guy slit her throat and dumped her body in the back of an alley. The unsettling thing about it was that the guy in question was one of my regulars.

From Porn to the Pulpit

One night a Caucasian guy emailed me and asked if I could meet him at a motel in L.A. When I got there he looked like *Jeffrey Dahmer* which instantly horrified me. I remained calm until he took his shirt off and I saw a big Nazi flag tattooed on his chest. He started talking about how much he hated black people and what they did to him when he was in prison. As he was talking he tied a rubber band around his arm while he prepared to shoot heroin in his vein. I was wondering why would he call a black prostitute if he hated black people. After he got high he started waving the syringe around. I thought he was going to stab me with it. Something in me said leave, so when he went into the bathroom I ran out of the motel room.

I went back to Hollywood. I was doing a few house calls that night. On my way into the last house I was stopped by a black Honda Accord. The man was Hispanic and he asked if I could talk to him for a second. I agreed because I already knew what he wanted. When I sat in his car he locked the door and sped off. He said, "I like little hookers like you, were gonna have a lot of fun!" I asked him to let me out of the car and he refused. He started reaching for something under his seat, but before he could get it I stabbed him in the hand. I jumped out of his car and ran like the wind.

Most women would have stopped prostituting after enduring all of that, but not me. I just grew a stronger hatred towards men. I wasn't going to stop hustling. I didn't care what they did to me. I was at a point in my life where I didn't love anything or anyone except money and drugs. I didn't care about myself, so why would anybody else care about me. I knew the life I led was going to come with some problems, but I felt it was worth the risk.

My biggest fear was not what those men could do to me physically, but what they could do to me sexually. I was terrified of catching H.I.V; more and more strippers and prostitutes were turning up positive. I was confident in thinking that it would never happen to me since I overly protected myself while prostituting. But my confidence went out the window when condoms started breaking. My heart stopped beating for a moment when I saw a broken condom after having sex with a total stranger. I never experienced real fear until that happened. Those three letters (H.I.V) scared me more than having a gun put to my head.

I decided to give Hollywood a break and I started

traveling more. One of my favorite places to go was St. Thomas Virgin Islands. It reminded me of my Caribbean background and I made a lot of money there. I was liked very much by the men and women. I loved the Island so much that I decided to stay, but drama followed me everywhere I went.

I started sleeping with the bouncer at the club I danced at. When we got involved with each other we had an understanding that it was just sex. But things changed when I caught feelings for him. I didn't realize it until I saw him flirting with the other strippers in the club. Before I knew it, I was more concerned about him rather than making money. I tried to control my emotions, but that didn't last long. I wanted to fight him and every girl I saw him with. We fought each other often, but the last straw was when he beat me up at the club in front of everybody.

When that was over I started seeing the captain of the police department. He was a handsome older man who was born and raised on the Island and he loved him some me. He paid me inside and outside of the club; we saw each other every day. He grew very fond of me and he would've given me the world if I asked for it. At first he was okay with me

Please Don't Kill Me

stripping and sleeping with men for money until he allowed his feelings to get the best of him. He wanted me all to himself, but that was not going to happen for two reasons. For one, I wasn't going to stop hustling for anybody and for two, he was married with kids. But he didn't seem to understand that. He would come in the club and intimidate my tippers. If he saw them talking to me he would threaten to arrest them. He showed up to my hotel room all hours of the night crying and begging to be with me. He told me he was going to leave his wife so we could get married. I've been proposed to many times from many different men, but this was a little different. I tried to avoid him, but St. Thomas isn't that big and it wasn't hard for him to find me. One day he saw me talking to a man at the beach. He walked over to me, whispered in my ear and said, "I'm the police you can come up missing real fast; don't play with me!"

After that he was everywhere controlling my every move; he watched me like a hawk. I was terrified of him because he was the captain of the police department which meant he carried a loaded gun at all times. I knew he could have really hurt me and no one would care or find out about it. I was uncomfortable being around him. I couldn't take it anymore, so I packed my bags and flew back to L.A.

I was ready to party and get my mind off the traumatic things that were going on around me. My longtime friend "Red" and I stayed at the club. Every other night we found somewhere to party. When we got together all hell would break loose; money, men, Xstacy, and a whole lot of alcohol. When we mixed all that together we became belligerent towards others. We never picked fights, but we sure finished them. That included knives and even gun play. Although we are women we couldn't shake that gangsta mentality. I never mentioned it to Red, but I feared for our lives. Fearing that if the drugs and alcohol didn't kill us one of the girls we fought with would. Retaliation is a big thing especially in Los Angeles. I just knew that somebody was going to catch us when we weren't paying attention.

I did catch one disease from the porn industry. I caught a murdering spirit from somebody I slept with. I always felt like I would have to kill them before they killed us and I was willing to take their lives if it meant saving mine or hers. Before walking into the club, also known as the pit of our enemies, I would pray that God wouldn't allow any hurt, harm, or danger to come to me or Red.

After being home for a while some way S.D got in touch with me. He asked if I could meet him at his shop in Inglewood. When we saw each other it brought back a lot of old feelings for him, not so much for me. I was already over him; my new love was for the game not S.D. He didn't see it that way. He called me all the time and wanted me to spend every night with him. He wanted things back the way they used to be, but I couldn't give him that. One night I was escorting and preparing to leave for New York the following day. S.D wanted to spend some time with me before I left and I agreed to meet with him after I finished my dates. He wanted me to drop everything right away, but I wasn't about to do that. Money always came first and he should've known that. The fact that I wasn't at his beck and call made him angry. He cursed me out, but I ignored him and continued on with my client. When I finished I headed over to S.D's shop. When I got there he was sitting on the couch. I sat next to him and asked, "What's the problem?" He didn't respond which made me angry and I cursed him out. He got up and slammed me into the wall. I slapped him; he pushed me to the floor and walked away. I thought our little tussle was over, but before I could get up he charged at me and hit me in the face with a long stem light bulb. The glass shattered cutting my head and face and then he started strangling me. As I was going in and out of consciousness all I could do was scream, "JESUS!!!" S.D replied by saying, "Jesus ain't in here." Then he spit in my face. I was about to pass out, but his brother walked in just in time and got him off of me. Trying to catch my breath I got off of the floor. I looked at him and said, "How could you?" With no remorse he told me to get out.

S.D and I went through a lot, but he never put his hands on me. We actually joked about it because he beat most of the women in his life except me, until now. Out of all the men who abused me it truly hurt me when S.D did it because I really cared about him. But my hurt turned into rage rapidly. I rushed to Red's house to get a gun. I was going to kill S.D, but for some reason Red wouldn't give me the gun. I guess she was being a good friend, but I was infuriated. Even though I was upset I wasn't going to let a couple of bumps and bruises stop me.

Please Don't Kill Me

I just wiped the blood off my face and applied rubbing alcohol to my scratches. I lay down and prepared myself to go to New York.

It was weird because everything was telling me not to go and not just because of the fight S.D and I had. A few days before I was getting ready to leave I was very indecisive which was unusual. Other people told me not to go too and no one has ever done that. Something definitely was not right, but despite how I felt or how anyone else felt I went anyway.

Chapter 11

New York

New York was a place that I've always wanted to go. I think most people do. Before I chose a life of porn and prostitution my dream was to go to New York University and study law. I've waited my whole life to get to this place. In August of 2008, the opportunity came my way and I jumped on it.

I was well known in multiple states and countries because of the dancing and porn. I networked a lot and I made myself accessible to be contacted by anybody anywhere. A Haitian man named "Bo"

From Porn To The Pulpit

from New York contacted me via internet. We talked over the phone and through email for over a month. He insisted that I come to New York right away. I told him that a porn director in New York contacted me a few days prior and asked if I'd be interested in shooting a few scenes for him. I said yes, but I had to wait for him to give me a date. Bo told me I could stay with him while I waited for the director and he would take care of all my expenses.

Bo was supposedly this big time A&R for a record label, he owned property all over New York. He had a traveling agency, a Lamborghini, and so on. Well, that was the information that he gave to me. I wasn't doubtful because I've done this with men plenty of times before and everything was legit. I assumed everything would be fine and I took a chance and went to see Bo.

When I arrived to Long Island, New York something wasn't right. I looked at my plane ticket and it was just a one way. There was no return ticket. I overlooked it and considered it to be a small mistake. I waited in the LaGuardia Airport for him to pull up in a Lamborghini, but there was no Lamborghini instead it was a Honda Accord. Once again, I overlooked it. I thought that maybe

New York

he just wanted to be discreet. (Hey, I tried to give the brother the benefit of the doubt.)

When we left the airport I expected him to take me to a beautiful house in the Hamptons or an exquisite hotel in Manhattan. Something to that extent, but we pulled up to an apartment in Brooklyn. Nothing about Brooklyn is luxurious whatsoever. I felt like I was still in Compton and now I'm confused and irritated. He told me that one of his homes was being rented, the other was being renovated, and the other one was too far. Even though his story wasn't adding up the apartment wasn't that bad and he gave me money when I got there, so I was okay at that point.

He took me to dinner and showed me a great time. He seemed like a really nice guy (at first). He treated me like I was his girlfriend which was common. Most of my clients caught feelings for me, but I knew what I was there for. I slept with him the first night which unfortunately increased his affection towards me. He became annoying wanting to be under me every two seconds. He introduce me to his friends as his "girl." I couldn't stand it, but I had to play the role because he was paying.

From Porn to the Pulpit

I didn't want to sit under him all day so we went to a few strip clubs to keep me occupied while I waited on the porn director to contact me for the scenes. After going to many strip clubs all throughout the Boroughs of NY I decided to dance at a club in the Bronx. I always made a lot of money when I danced, especially when I was special guest, but for some reason it didn't happen here. I danced two nights in a row and barely made one thousand dollars which was absolutely abnormal for me. I didn't get discouraged. I'd been in the game for five and a half years and I knew how to make money. I got a few numbers from the guys that were in there, so I could see them outside of the club.

The next night Bo wanted us to go have fun at a night club in Manhattan. The club was packed and I was enjoying myself, but I was there for one reason and one reason only, MONEY! I snuck away from Bo and introduced myself to a few men in the club and exchanged numbers with them. I didn't think Bo saw me since the club was so crowded, but he definitely saw me and became enraged.

While I was in the middle of a conversation with a guy Bo snatched me out of the club and we started arguing. I had a horrible way with words

New York

and I never backed down from an argument. I told him I didn't know why he was so mad I wasn't his girl. This was business that's it. I guess that was the wrong thing to say because he kicked me out of his car and drove off. It was four in the morning and I was somewhere in Manhattan wearing a little black dress with a pair of gold heels. I was so upset and I was in a hurry to get out of there. I decided to catch a taxi to the J.F.K Airport and catch the next flight to L.A.X. I didn't care that my suitcases were in his car I was ready to go, immediately. Before a taxi could pull up Bo came back. He told me to get in his car and I said no! He drove the car on the sidewalk so I couldn't pass by. He got out, punched me in my face, and pulled me into the car by my hair. I tried to get out, but the doors were locked. He hit me again and said, "You messed with the wrong one. I bet you won't leave here now!"

At that very moment an indescribable fear kicked in because I had no control over the situation. I was on the East Coast with no family, no friends, no enemies, no one. It was just me and him. I had no idea what this man was about to do to me.

He drove faster and faster on the interstate. I started crying while he laughed and mocked me.

From Porn to the Pulpit

We pulled up to an old raged house that looked haunted and abandoned. I refused to get out of the car, so Bo came to the passenger side and pulled me out. He made me walk to the back of the house where the basement was located. The basement was large in size, but it had a room in the corner smaller than a jail cell. It had a twin size mattress, an old television, no window; it was pitch black dark, and filthy. It looked like a dungeon where you torture people. I had never seen anything like this in my life. Still having an attitude I said, "I'm not staying here." Bo pushed me in the room and locked the door. I was a little intoxicated from the drinks we had at the club, so it seemed like a bad dream that I would awaken from, but this was no dream.

I fell asleep, but I woke up when he came back to the basement later that night to have sex with me which was very unpleasant. He was extremely rough and aggressive, but I was relieved when he finished shortly after he began. He lay beside me and wrapped his arm around me with a tight grip making sure I couldn't move. He was also into voodoo. When he thought I was sleeping he would lay over me and chant. I don't know what type of spell he wanted to put on me. I thought that he was

New York

going to use me as a sacrifice to the devil.

As the days went by he got weirder, angrier and crazier. He would wake me up, sit me in a chair, and cry in front of me as he reminisced about his father and how things were not going right for him. This just further confused me and I started to feel sorry for him because I didn't know if he was a psycho, Bipolar, or Schizophrenic. Whatever it was he was crazy. This became an everyday routine for three weeks. I was only supposed to be in New York for a few days.

The most frightening thing of it all was the whole time I was in that basement his mother and her twenty cats were living upstairs. She heard me scream, yell and cry night after night and yet she did absolutely nothing. She saw me when Bo sent me upstairs to take showers. I tried to make eye contact with her so she could see that something was wrong, but she intentionally turned the other cheek. Although she was Haitian and didn't speak very much English I'm convinced that anybody no matter what language they speak understands screaming and hollering. She never asked or came down there to see what her son was doing to me as if this was something he did on a regular basis.

From Porn to the Pulpit

While I was in there I had a lot of time to think and I became so displeased with myself as I realized that I was about to lose my life because of dumb decisions I made. All this for money and drugs, porn and prostitution. I couldn't be mad at anybody but myself, I did this. I chose to come out here with him. If I'd never chosen this life I wouldn't be in his basement. I've always heard that the fast life will get you in one of two places, dead or in jail. I remembered how I continually stated that the only way for me to get out of the game is if I died.

I even prayed for death and God answers prayers. The Bible says death and life are in the power of the tongue. (Proverbs 18:21) I spoke death over my life and it's really happening. I'm in a situation where I'm about to die and in the most horrible way you could imagine. Bo could have cut my body into pieces and buried me in his backyard. Who would have known? The only information my family and friends had was that I was somewhere in New York. As the days went on I just reminisced on my life and how I ended up here.

After being raped, beaten, and abused mentally, physically, and emotionally, I had totally given up

New York

on life. When he came to the basement once a day to feed me he told me over and over again that he should kill me and that I wasn't going to leave. He told me how worthless I was and after a while I started believing it. There was no fight left in me there was no hope. I became so stressed out my whole body began to hurt. I wasn't eating regularly; I tried to overdose off my Prozac pills. I wasn't sleeping, I was mentally unstable, my fake hair started falling out, I just became a lost soul. It seemed like he was turned on by my misery, the sadder I became the happier he got. I just gave all power to him. When he wanted sex I wouldn't fight, when he talked down to me I wouldn't respond, when he hit me I took every blow. I literally gave up on any chance of survival. My life was now over at age nineteen and I accepted death.

One thing he did allow me to do was accept phone calls from my mom and grandma. I guess he figured that since I was never going to see them again I could at least talk to them. He stood right there and I had to pretend like everything was okay. My grandmother asked me when was I coming home since it had already been three weeks. I lied and said that I was having such a good time and I didn't know when I was coming back. Every time I heard her voice without her knowing I would weep because I really believed that I would never see her again. Just knowing that was enough to make me crumble; my grandparents mean a lot to me.

For so many years I had become numb and careless because of all the drugs I was consuming, but being sober in that basement made me realize how much I really loved my family. I just wanted to go home and hug them and tell them I love them. After hanging up with my grandmother Bo left the basement and I cried uncontrollably. I have no idea how I ended up on that filthy floor, but I laid there and hollered for hours. I was so discombobulated I couldn't talk. After taking a few deep breaths I finally got my words together and began to speak. Out of nowhere something in me just said, "Pray Danielle." I told God, "If You get me out of this I'll change my life for You. I will never do this again I promise. Please don't let me die like this, please!!!"

I know I lied to Him before, but from the bottom of my soul I meant it this time. If I made it out of this there was no way in hell that I would go back. I

New York

stayed in a fetal position and talked to Him for hours. I was in much need of a second chance.

Approximately two or three days later Bo's Jamaican friend came to the basement to pick up a package. (He and Bo sold drugs.) He heard me making noise in the corner; he opened the door and saw my condition. He walked over to me and said, "Yo shorty, you alright?" When I told him what Bo was doing to me he held me in his arms and told me he was sorry that I had to go through this; he had no idea that Bo was like that. He told me that Bo no longer worked for the record label, he didn't own any property, the money that he used to have was from his father's death, and that money was gone a long time ago. In fact, the Brooklyn apartment I was staying in was not his either it was all a lie. Now I felt like a fool. He did all this to me and he's broke! Bo's friend called me a taxi and after three weeks of the basement I was finally free or at least that's what I thought…

Once I got in the taxi I was relieved that I was out of the basement and away from Bo, but I didn't know where I was going to go. I knew no one. When I first arrived in New York I was stripping at a club in the Bronx and I met a few guys. I started calling around to see where I could go. I called the bouncer that worked at the strip club. He told me to meet him at his second job. He worked at a bar in Manhattan. When I got there I waited for him to get off then we headed to his apartment. I stayed there for a few days and thought about how I was going to leave NY. My stay there was fine until he told me his girlfriend was coming back home from her trip. He told me he would take me wherever I needed to go. I asked him to drop me off at a motel in Queens. I had enough money for a motel room but not a plane ticket. My plans were to stay at the motel and escort until I got enough money to leave. But it didn't work out that way. After two days the motel money ran out.

I thought long and hard about my next move which was frustrating because I was stranded in New York with no money. Not having any other options I just bounced from stranger to stranger who wanted sex from me every second.

I was so desperate to get out of New York. I had truly hit a low point, so much that I would have "worked" on the streets if I would've found out where the track was located. I met a prostitute who was willing to go with me, but she had a pimp. I

New York

was not about to get caught up in that again.

I called another guy that I met while I was dancing. He agreed to let me stay with him at his house in Yonkers. When I got there I was actually comfortable, he was such a gentlemen. He didn't ask me for sex and he really tried to help me, but he wanted me to be his girlfriend and that wasn't going to happen. I was trying to get out of New York not start a relationship.

I was so traumatized that I forgot about the porn director I was supposed to meet up with to do the scenes. I called and explained my situation to him he told me to have a taxi bring me to Harlem where he was. When I arrived in Harlem, "Big Moe" showed up an hour late in his Benz. He jumped out, paid the taxi driver, and told me to get in his car. I only met Big Moe twice prior to this time. Once in Las Vegas at the AVN Porn Convention then at the Urban Spice Awards in L.A and both times I didn't like him very much. He was arrogant, cocky, and rude, but he offered me work that's why I kept in touch with him. Although this time he seemed to be much nicer than before. He told me I could stay at his guest house which was also in Yonkers and he would shoot some scenes for me so I could get enough money to get back home.

I truly meant it when I told God I was going to change, but I was still in New York and I had to do what I had to do to survive while I was there. I decided to do the scenes just to get enough money to get home and then I was going to stop completely. When I arrived to the guest house it was beautiful. Big Moe showed me to my room and assured me that everything would be okay he was there to help.

As long as I'd been in the game I knew that these kinds of people didn't just do things out of the kindness of their hearts. It was always an ulterior motive behind the kindness. I wasn't surprised when he told me what was expected of me for him "helping me." He wanted sex and not just regular sex, but kinky, perverted, animalistic, disgusting, nasty sex, and it went from a want to a mandatory thing for my stay at his house. Since I had nowhere else to go I cooperated.

Big Moe wasn't an attractive man at all he was very large and hairy which made it even more difficult. The things he asked me to do to him turned my stomach, literally. I vomited multiple times in the middle of the act. He would also bring

New York

different girls off the street to the house for me to sleep with in front of him for his entertainment.

Most of the girls were under eighteen. I was nineteen at the time and Big Moe was pushing fifty. He liked them young and I do mean young. This perversion went on every night while I was there. I did a few porn scenes for his company in the daytime then slept with him and whoever else he decided to bring home at night.

At that point I realized that I had become his sex slave. Anything I wanted or needed I had to have sex for. I needed some where to stay, had to have sex; I needed money, had to have sex. I needed food, had to have sex; I wanted to go somewhere, had to have sex. I began to hate sex even the word made my skin crawl. Sex became my enemy; something that I once enjoyed became sickening to me. It was being used to destroy me. I couldn't take it anymore as the days went by I grew angrier and irrational. Big Moe and I began to argue a lot because he didn't like my attitude and I didn't like him at all.

He came to the house with two young girls; they were no older than seventeen. We started arguing because he left me in the house all day with no food and all he wanted to do was have sex with me and under aged girls. I went outside and sat on the patio while Big Moe and the two girls were getting ready to engage in their ridiculous sexual adventures. The longer I sat there the more uncontainable my anger and frustration became, so I did what I knew best. I took a chair and threw it at the glass door and the door shattered. Big Moe ran outside and saw the shattered glass. He was furious and started walking towards me as if he wanted to hit me. I wanted him to hit me because I had a knife in my pocket and my plan was to stab him, take his money, and buy me a plane ticket. But he didn't hit me. He just threw my bags out and told me I had to leave which was great. After a week and a half of torment the perverted sexual abuse was over.

Throughout all of this I was conversing with a guy named "Kidd" that I also met at the strip club. I told him everything that was happening with Big Moe and he suggested that I stay with him in Harlem and he would take care of me without all the extras. I argued nonstop with Big Moe until he dropped me off in Harlem. When I got there I called Kidd to come get me. He picked me up and took me to dinner. He told me that everything

New York

would be okay and I wanted to believe him. I desperately needed for everything to be okay.

Kidd was humongous. He was 6'6 and close to three hundred pounds, but he had money and he made me laugh. He took my mind off of every negative thing that was happening. For a second, I thought that he really wanted to help me. The first three days were great. He took me shopping, he gave me money; he bought me Xstacy. (After everything that was happening to me I anticipated on getting high.) Things were better than I could imagine until after the third day.

He felt that he deserved to be rewarded for being so good to me which of course included sex. That really annoyed me because I explained to him what just happened to me. Even if I wanted to have sex with him, (which I didn't) I was in no condition to have sex with anyone I was all sexed out. He couldn't care less he wanted sex and that was that. I said no and he laughed like I was joking, but when he saw that I was serious he became irate with me. He started calling me names; "Porno Hoe" was his favorite. After a few hours of name calling, the hitting began.

I have been in many abusive situations with men

before, but this time was the absolute worst. Kidd was a very big man and when he hit me it felt like a building fell on me. The first time he slapped me, but I fought back. Then he started throwing me through things, like the wall, tables, and through doors. I still didn't have sex with him. I didn't care what he did to me I was not going to sleep with him!

He turned it up a notch. He stopped feeding me; he wouldn't buy any food. I was starving and became weak which intensified the hits ten times more, but I still would not sleep with this man. He decided to take it a step further; he started beating me with things. He hit me with a skillet, my stilettos, his belt, or whatever he could find. I remember asking him, "If you want it that bad why won't you take it?" He said he shouldn't have to take it I should want to give it to him. But that was the thing. I didn't want to give it to him he could have killed me and even in my death I still wouldn't sleep with him.

The abuse continued and I found the rest of the Xstacy pills that he bought me. Since I was starving the pills would take my appetite away and numb me from the pain of him beating me. I took the last

New York

three pills then Kidd walked in and tried to apologize to me, but I knew that this was just another one of his plots to keep me there, so he could have sex with me. He saw that I wasn't buying it and it frustrated him even more. He tried so many ways to "get me" and sadly none of it was working. So once again here comes the pain. He didn't know that I took the pills and was numb, so every time he hit me I looked at him with a smirk and said, "Are you done yet?"

He left me in the apartment a few more hours and my sobriety kicked in. I realized that Kidd was probably going to beat me to death. I had to get out of this, but how? I cried and asked God to get me out of there this can't be how my life is going to end, it just can't be. After I gathered my thoughts I realized that I had a guy friend in New Jersey named "Shinobi," but I couldn't remember his number. I just started dialing and by Grace the third try was his. When he answered the phone my heart dropped, I was so happy. I told him everything that happened and his response was,

"Just get to Jersey and I'll take care of the rest." He told me to catch the train in Manhattan, but I had no money and no way out of Kidd's apartment. But what I did have was determination. I was determined to survive by any means necessary! I woke up the next morning to Kidd standing over me. He was mad because I slept in another room and locked him out. He tried to talk to me, but I didn't want to hear what he had to say. He began hitting me, but this time I had the strength of ten bears. I jumped on him and went to work! We fought like Tyson and Holyfield that morning. (I just didn't bite his ear off for fear of catching something.) Eventually, he overpowered me and threw me to the floor. As he was coming towards me with full force I saw a knife in my reach. I grabbed it and stabbed him in his shoulder. I grabbed my bag and ran out the door. I stood in the middle of the street hoping a taxi would come get me before Kidd did. The taxi stopped and I had a bloody knife in my hand, but instead of him driving off or calling the police on me he offered to take me to the train station. Before I could get in the taxi Kidd came running towards me holding his bloody shoulder.

He said, "Ima kill you!"

I turned to him with the knife still in my hand and said, "If you touch me the next thing bleeding will be your throat."

New York

Kidd didn't come any closer I got in the taxi and we drove off. I told the driver I didn't have any money, but I was willing to do whatever he wanted if he would just take me to the train. He told me it was okay I didn't have to do anything. When I got to the train station my clothes were torn, I had bumps and bruises on my face, and I still had Kidd's blood on my hands, but I was ecstatic. I was finally free from hell, a.k.a New York.

I arrived in Edison, New Jersey where Shinobi lived, and unlike the others he made me feel so secure. For once, I was around a man who was helping me not because of ulterior motives, but because he actually cared. The fact that he used to be a Pastor was even better; he had just backslidden when he met me. It was definitely a Divine connection for the both of us because after he saw everything I went through he got back involved with ministry and I was ready to run to Jesus and never look back. I stayed with him and his family for a few days then he purchased me a plane ticket back to L.A. After a whole month and a half of New York it was finally over.

Chapter 12

God Help Me!

The plane ride home was exciting I was so happy! It was by Grace and Mercy alone that I made it out alive. When the pilot announced that we were about to land at L.A.X Airport reality kicked in. I had a brand new 2008 truck, an apartment and a lifestyle I was accustomed to, but because of the promise I made to God I had to give it all up and I did!

I walked away from the porn industry. I didn't dance anymore, I stopped sleeping with men for money, and because of it I lost my apartment. I

could no longer pay for it. I packed all of my belongings and put them into my truck. Unfortunately, my truck was stolen that same night. Everything I owned was in there, my clothes, my shoes, my purses, and my jewelry. I literally was left with only the clothes on my back. I couldn't live the lavish lifestyle with no money. I had nothing left because I never saved and I spent money on a daily basis. I didn't see the need to save since I was constantly making money. I really believed that I was going to be a prostitute for the rest of my
life.

Most people would have gone crazy after losing everything they've "worked" for, but I was so happy to be alive, none of that stuff mattered. (At first) I also asked God for a new beginning, so when I began losing things I knew that it was Him giving me what I asked for. We all should know that we don't keep things that we get the wrong way.
(Proverbs 13:11 Wealth gained by dishonesty will be diminished, but he who gathers by labor will increase.)

I was in church every Sunday and Wednesday. I thought I was pleasing God because I left the porn

God Help Me!

industry and stopped prostituting like I told Him. But I was still taking X pills, going to the club every other night, and sleeping with a lot of men and women. (I just wasn't getting paid for it.) I didn't forgive the people who hurt me, I was still fighting, I was still getting drunk; I was still a hot mess. But because I stopped one of the major things in my life and was in church regularly I thought everything was okay and sadly that's what most Christians believe. We'll stop doing a few things and go to church a little more then we expect to go to Heaven. Sorry, but that's absolutely, positively untrue.
(Matthew 7:21 Not everyone who says to me Lord, Lord shall enter the kingdom of Heaven, but he who does the will of my Father in Heaven.)

Most people don't know or don't care like me. I didn't know that I was doing anything wrong. I actually became very upset with God. I didn't understand how I turned my life around for Him and yet nothing was coming out of it. I was so fixed on the fact that I walked away from the most addicting thing in my life for Him. I went to church every Sunday, (before going to the club) and I started reading my Bible. (While drinking Jose Cuervo. I couldn't understand the King James

Version unless I was tipsy.) I wasn't perfect, but I kept my end of the bargain and He didn't. What's up with that? While I was complaining He spoke to me and simply said, "I want all of you."

No matter how I tried to sugarcoat it I realized that what I was doing wasn't right and He wanted me to stop, but I couldn't. I couldn't stop drinking because I was an alcoholic and I couldn't stop doing drugs because it helped me to deal with the pain I was feeling. I liked to fight because I was angry and that's how I dealt with my problems. But what God did for me would always come to mind. I remembered how I should've died, but He didn't let me. I should've caught a disease, but He didn't allow it. He saw something in me to keep me alive and that was enough for me to try my best to make a change.

As many times as I tried to stop everything I knew that I couldn't do it on my own. I tried numerous times with no success. I've always known that there is power in prayer, so I sincerely prayed for help to stop doing drugs, sleeping with women, fighting people, going to the club, drinking, messing with so many guys, and the process began.

God Help Me!

It seemed like it happened overnight because my desire quickly changed for a lot of things. Most people go to counseling or AA meetings to help them to stop drinking or doing drugs, but I simply asked God to take it away and He did! I didn't have the same taste for it anymore. I didn't want to get high or drunk ever again. I had no interest in going to a club. I stopped messing with women completely. I woke up one morning and didn't view them the same way. When I looked at a female there were no more lustful thoughts. I wasn't attracted to them at all. I was on the right track and believed that I made a complete turnaround. I became very proud of myself almost to the point of boastfulness.

I saw a small change, but not much which really confused me. I said, "Lord You trippin'! I stopped everything for You what's the problem?"

Again, He said, "I want all of you."

He revealed to me what my problem was. I was a lukewarm Christian. I honored Him with my lips, but my heart was far from Him. I was very unforgiving; I was sleeping with a man I wasn't married to. I was very angry towards my parents and I said I was a new person, but I still had that old mentality. (Queen B wasn't dead yet.) I didn't like or love the person I saw in the mirror. My anger shifted from others onto myself. I became my worst enemy because I was ashamed of the things I chose to do.

First of all, how could I forgive all of those men who hurt me especially my father? They damaged me for life and I wanted them all to pay. I would fantasize of ways to torture them if I ever got my chance for revenge. They hurt me, they scarred me, and I couldn't let it go. I was extremely angry because life made me that way. All the pain, turmoil, and disappointments that life put me through you better believe I was angry. I had not one, but two parents who couldn't care less about my wellbeing. I became envious of the relationships my friends had with their parents because I wanted the same thing. I fought so much because people knew how to kindle my fire, so they got burned. I stopped my promiscuous ways and settled down with one (abusive) man who promised to marry me once he got divorced from his wife whom he was separated from. And yes, I am a new person Queen just talks to me every now and then.

As I got closer to Christ, conviction started to

God Help Me!

penetrate me. The Holy Spirit led me to the scripture in Luke 5:37-38, about old wineskins and new wineskins. I related to it because I was doing new things, but I was operating with an old mindset. I tried to convince myself that I wasn't doing anything wrong, but in reality I was doing everything wrong. I didn't know how to be a Christian and I was negotiating with God. I believed because I left the porn industry and stopped stripping I was pleasing Him, but in reality I was slapping Him in the face. He saved me from death and I'm repaying Him with my foolishness.

When I realized what I was doing I cried out and said, "GOD HELP ME!" I needed and wanted Him to sincerely transform my life. I was getting tired of the life I was living anyway, all the drama, depression, anger, fighting, etc. I knew there had to be more to life than this. I was ready to let go and let God have full control.

In order to go through my transformation I had to let the married guy go which wasn't too hard. He caused me a great deal of heartache. He too was physically and mentally abusive. But I stayed for two reasons. (1) I had become accustomed to abuse and believed in my mind that it was normal. Sadly, that's all I've been exposed to my whole life. I didn't know anything other than violence and mistreatment. (2) I stayed with him so long because of our sexual history. Sex was the head of our relationship and when sex (not love, just sex) is involved it alters your right way of thinking. The physical/sexual connection can be stronger than anything else if you allow it. But after asking God to destroy that soul tie we were over.

I disconnected myself from a lot of "friends" who were still stripping and doing porn. I knew that this transformation would be hard if I did it alone, but it was ten times harder with them around me. They didn't encourage my change. In fact they tried anything and everything to get me back into that lifestyle. The more I tried to walk away from it the more they tried to pull me back into it. If they couldn't persuade me with porn and stripping they would use drugs and alcohol. I was determined to walk this path of righteousness, so I cut off anything that would be a hindrance including them.

(2 Corinthians 6:14-17 Do not be unequally yoked together with unbelievers…Come out from among them, and be separate, says the Lord.)

God Help Me!

The next thing I had to do was change my old way of thinking. Queen disappeared, but she wasn't dead yet. She was just on vacation. She would pop up from time to time to remind me how to dress and not to mess with broke or financially challenged men. Although I physically stopped prostituting mentally I was still a prostitute. I would only date the gangsters, hit men, and drug dealers who had the nice cars and the money. It's a sad and demoralizing thing for a woman to need something like money or men to fulfill her. To fix this, I just stopped dating men altogether until I prayed for God to help me change my way of thinking. Slowly but surely, I didn't focus on where a man was financially, but I paid more attention to where he was spiritually.

I was also ready to forgive. It wasn't easy, but I had to do it. I thought about all the pain I caused the Lord with my actions and I wanted Him to forgive me. I knew there was no way that He would forgive me if I refused to forgive somebody else. I didn't want to allow those people to still have a hold over my life. I realized that forgiveness wasn't condoning what they did to me, but it would set me free once I finally released it. When you choose to not forgive people it can make you sick and bitter. And as you continue your days with hatred in your heart in the end you will lose.

Now the hardest part for me was letting go of the anger. I let go of a lot, a whole lot, but that anger wouldn't go anywhere. Anger was definitely my stronghold. It actually scared me at times because when I became angry I lost all control. I would black out and become another person. I became my father. Anger had taken control of my life for so long. I realized that anger came from hurt, but I was ready for it to go away. I cried out to Him and said, "Please help me Lord. I can't do this by myself. I don't want to be an angry person, but I don't know how to let it go."

It went from a 10 to a 3. It wasn't as bad as before, but it was still there. It was there because even though I prayed for Him to take it away I wanted to use it when necessary. My mouth said I wanted it gone, but my heart said something else. I still had that gangster mentality and I was big on respect. If you disrespected me I would act like a psychotic maniac. Now is that what God wants? Absolutely not. The first step to your breakthrough is realizing and admitting that you have a problem. I realized

God Help Me!

that my anger and attitude was an issue, and once I addressed it God started to break it.

At this time I was attending a church in Bellflower. I was at the Altar every Sunday and Tuesday for months until I got what I came for, my deliverance. It was very painful as God started to remove the layers off of me. Deliverance can be the hardest thing a person will ever go through. I cried, I screamed, I was uncomfortable, I lost everything. I really went through it. It felt as if I was watching myself die and that's exactly what was happening. That old man was dying and I felt every bit of it. While hands were being laid on me and the demonic spirits were being cast out of me, my life seemed to take a turn for the worst. God stripped me of everything! There was nothing left, but through the tears I refused to give up. At that time all I had was Jesus, so I just went through it and I was willing to do whatever it took.

While the deliverance was taken place I became isolated and focused all of my attention on Christ. I grew an interest in reading the Bible and praying more. I grew so much spiritually and He began to speak to me. He told me that I had purpose and destiny which was hard for me to accept. I was an ex-porn star what purpose could I possibly have? I tried to ignore it. For a second I thought I was going crazy because I kept hearing a Voice. Then I started having dreams; I saw myself on a platform in front of thousands of people. I told my mentor Pastor Jarvis Hines and he told me that God was going to use me for the Kingdom. He always tried to uplift my spirit, but I didn't receive it. The devil would always tell me, "How could God use you, you're a whore. You're not good enough, who will listen to you?" I started to believe the lying vanities that whispered in my ear, but Pastor Jarvis would always say, "The devil is a lie! You are somebody and God will use you to change lives."

But I didn't want that, I just wanted to be a "regular" Christian. I wanted to live for God and be obedient, that's it. I didn't want to be used to do anything; I didn't want to change or save any lives. I was okay with sitting on the pew. I was comfortable right where I was. I doubted myself more than other people did. I just couldn't make any sense out of it. I was (keyword, was) a prostitute, a drug addict, a lesbian, a stripper, an everything. Why would God choose me?

For some reason I couldn't shake it. The more I

God Help Me!

tried to ignore it the more it bothered me. I couldn't sleep, I couldn't think, I couldn't function properly without ministry being on my mind. I was in a mental battle with God. I would tell Him, "I'm not doing it." He would say, "Oh yes you are!" Knowing and understanding that I would never overpower the Lord I eventually gave up on my fight. I'm a strong believer in prayer. I prayed and asked the Lord, "Is it true, do You want to use me for ministry?"

He simply replied with a yes!

"How can You use me? After all the wrong I've done, why me? Who's gonna listen to me, who am I supposed to talk to? What am I supposed to do?"

He said, "I chose you now all you have to do is trust Me."

Even though I heard God's Voice and His assurance I still ran. I didn't want to do ministry. That was not on my agenda. I wanted to get my life right with Him, go to church, pay my tithes, and be a good person. That's it. I wanted nothing to do with other people, especially church people. I quickly found out that you can't tell God what you're not going to do. I tried to run and the more I ran, the more problems I had. Nothing went right for me. Every door was shut in my face; I had no happiness. I was stressed out and my prayers were hindered. It was bad on every side until I chose to obey. I finally said not my will, but Your will be done I'll do it.

I had no other choice, but to submit and commit my life to Christ. He was the only one that I trusted, so if He said ministry then ministry it was. I stopped running and I told the devil it was over! I'm done with you you're a liar! For once in my life I had something I never had before…peace. I professed that as long as I have Jesus I don't need nothing or nobody else. The money was gone, the cars were gone, the friends were gone, but I was finally happy.

When I had all that worldly stuff I was miserable. I had material things and that didn't make me happy.
(Matthew 16:26 For what profit is it to a man if he gains the whole world and loses his own soul?)

I was living a life filled with peace, joy, and happiness. I had something that nobody could ever take from me and that's my relationship with Christ. I obeyed Him and I accepted the call on my life. God began to speak to me more. He told me

God Help Me!

that I was chosen. He was going to use me to help other men and women who had been through some of the same things as I did. I had come into the knowledge of who I am and Who's I am. I was completely sold out for Jesus and ready to work for the Kingdom. This was my chance to pay my vows to Him. He saved my life and all I had to do was obey. I knew He called me to ministry too bad no one else did. Here comes the pain.

Chapter 13

The Breakdown

I made the mistake in thinking that once I got saved, sanctified, and Holy Ghost filled everything would be pretty pink roses. Um, not! All kinds of hell broke loose. I thought I was on the right track. I studied my Bible from Genesis to Revelation, I went to church four or five times a week, I prayed every day, I was sober, I became celibate, I surrounded myself with Godly people. At first everything was great. I didn't have a worry in the world until the devil saw that I was serious about my walk with Christ. Oh honey, you want to talk about pain and suffering.

From Porn to the Pulpit

I knew I had a not so great past, but God told me He was going to use me because of my past. He called me to ministry. He told me that I was a part of the Kingdom, but others didn't see it that way. So many people came against me, they talked about me, they laughed at me, and they told me I could never be a Minister. Everybody thought I was a joke. Worldly people said I was a sell out because I changed my life. I decided to do the right thing, so that meant I was fake and confused about who I am.

They gave my newfound faith a time limit. They were certain that I would be right back in the streets. I would often hear the famous quote, "Once a hoe always a hoe."

Church people looked at me with disgust because I didn't fit in. I didn't look like them, I didn't act like them, and I was younger than them. They were aware of my background, so in their eyes I was still a whore, but now I'm just a church whore. If they saw me conversing with a man at church they assumed that I was trying to sleep with him. I wasn't able to hug a man without somebody saying something about it. The women didn't want me to talk to their husbands at all. In their minds I was a

The Breakdown

Jezebel sent to destroy the marriages in the church. I didn't want those men. I just wanted to get closer to Jesus, but my spiritual needs didn't matter because of my reputation.

A Pastor told me that I wasn't called it was the devil telling me to preach, not God. I wasn't accepted anywhere, not in church or in the streets. I couldn't comprehend how Christ, someone that I cannot see treated me better than other "Christ-like" people who I can see.

My own family didn't take me seriously. I wanted their approval and acceptance so bad, but I was never good enough to get it. I would hear, "Oh that's good you changed, keep it up." But they'd still make little comments about what I used to do. I got so tired of hearing, "I remember when you…" That was the problem. They remembered so much of what I used to do that they couldn't see what I was doing now. No matter how hard I tried they still were not convinced. It was a lose/lose situation with them. When I was prostituting and selling drugs they didn't like that; now that I've changed my life for the better they still didn't approve. I could never please them no matter what I decided to do.

From Porn to the Pulpit

I took on this new identity. I completely blocked out my past and focused on the future, but for some reason my past wouldn't stay behind me. It wouldn't leave me alone. Everywhere I went someone recognized me from the movies or the clubs I danced in. I was in a mall and a guy yelled loudly, "Hey I know you, you do porn! I watched you last night." The shame and embarrassment nearly killed me.

One afternoon I was walking to a store and a Filipino guy that used to be my regular customer saw me and turned his car around. I told him I didn't escort anymore I was in church and I changed my life. After I said that he still asked if I wanted to go with him to his house. As hard as it was, (and it was hard) I said no. It was hard because he had money, a lot of it and at that time I didn't have anything.

Porn directors and strip clubs from all over the world were emailing me more than ever. They were offering me large amounts of money to come back. I would be a liar if I said I didn't think about going back all the time; especially when I didn't have any money. Every time I considered going back I would have a flashback of the basement. If that wasn't

The Breakdown

enough, God told me that I would die if I ever stepped back into a strip club or a porn set. What kept me from doing it was my fear of hurting God again and knowing that if I had gone back I would never come out. Even though I was well aware of the outcome that didn't stop me from wanting that life- style/money again. I had to fight with myself and beg God for His strength to keep me. But it was becoming a bit overwhelming.

I visited many churches and the men I slept with for money were sitting on the same pew with me. I couldn't praise God the way I wanted to because their stares made me uncomfortable. No matter where I went, whether church, malls, movie theaters, airports, restaurants, I kept seeing the people I slept with. They were everywhere! When I saw them I would run behind something, so they wouldn't see me. I tried to hide myself under big hoodies and sunglasses. I didn't want to engage in any conversations about what I used to do. I just wanted my past to disappear. I wanted to believe that it never happened.

I tried to be celibate and still date. That didn't work for obvious reasons, but I tried it anyway. I found out that the men I was dating were only interested in me because they saw the movies I was in. They didn't care about me as a person; they just wanted me to fulfill their fantasies. I explained to them over and over I'm not going to have sex with anybody and if I did it wouldn't be like that. Those were movies; I didn't really do those things in my personal life. I was acting. The celibate dating didn't work at all. My feelings were getting hurt because I was giving them Danielle, but they wanted Queen B.

Friends that I helped for years acted as if I no longer existed because I didn't have any more money. I did a lot for people. I gave money, clothes, food, and helped pay rent. I always went above and beyond for my friends. Anything they needed I gave it. I was there for them financially and emotionally. I just knew that they would help me when I needed them, but that wasn't the case. When I lost my car I called them to get a ride to work, but they refused to take me. I had no food and they wouldn't buy me a 99 cent cheeseburger. I needed a place to lay my head, but they refused to let me stay with them. I wasn't good enough to even sleep on their floor. I was no longer important because I couldn't support them anymore.

The Breakdown

The reality of being broke kicked in. When I first came home from New York I didn't focus on finances because I was so happy to be alive. Now that the happiness from having my life was over the fact that I was broke stressed me out. I never grew up poor, my mother, my father, and my grandparents all had good jobs. I started hustling at the age of fourteen, so I wasn't accustomed to not having things. I was miserable when I couldn't pay for food. I was riding the bus and wearing "hand me down" clothes. My misery quickly turned into depression. I sat at the bus stop and tears would roll down my face as the cars passed by. It hurt to see other people shopping when I had to wear second hand clothes. There would be days that I would starve because I was too ashamed to tell people I had no money to feed myself. The thought of having everything to having nothing was unendurable. I was embarrassed.

It seemed like my body was breaking down on me. I guess all the porn and prostituting finally caught up with me. Even though I was celibate at the time I was experiencing excruciating vaginal pain. It was so bad that I couldn't walk, I couldn't sit, I couldn't move. The pain was worse than before. I started passing out and having seizures again which made absolutely no sense because I was sober for over a year. I gained a large amount of weight. I was close to two hundred pounds because I ate my way through the depression.

The ex-boyfriend decided that he was going to harass me daily. He didn't understand why I couldn't continue sleeping with a married man or sleeping with anybody at all. He called and cursed me out every day. He was a thug and this was how he dealt with his feelings. The funny thing was he wasn't upset about me not wanting to have sex. He was upset because I didn't want to be with him. I guess the rejection didn't sit well with him, so the harassing calls kept coming.

I ignored the issues in my personal life because I was happy when I finally found a new job. I was working there for a few months and someone decided to bring a porno with me on the front cover. Not only did he bring it to work he showed every employee there. Management heard about it and fired me. Of course they didn't tell me the real reason why they let me go, but I knew why. This devastated me. I could deal with people talking about me, I could deal with the crazy ex-boyfriend,

The Breakdown

I could even deal with the fake friends who turned their back on me, but this was a little too much to handle.

I was humiliated, embarrassed, and hurt to an unexplainable level. All I kept screaming was, "WHY, GOD WHY? How could You let this happen to me?"

He said, "It's ok just trust Me."

It's hard to trust God when all hell has broken loose. "How can I trust You when everything is falling apart?" I had no money, I had no job, I had nothing. I lost my friends and my body was hurting. My life was crumbling right in front of me.

Pain was something that I was a little too familiar with. Everything I thought I was healed from snuck up on me. I was hurting from the things I was going through at that moment, but in actuality I was still hurting from everything I went through in my past too. I was hurt because I couldn't figure out why my parents didn't love me the way I needed them to. I was hurting because I didn't know why men chose to rape and beat me. I was hurting because I was still traumatized from what happened in New York. I was hurting because I made a decision to do porn and it backfired. I was hurting because everyone who told me they loved me disappointed me in one way or another.

It took all these things to happen for me to realize that I wasn't completely healed. Even though God spoke to me and revealed things to me I was still in pain. I was Anointed and afflicted at the same time. I tried to pray, but the words wouldn't come out. I went to church and though I was there physically I wasn't there spiritually or mentally. God didn't have my undivided attention anymore. All I thought about was my heartache. My church family tried to encourage me, but my pain wouldn't allow me to hear their words. I viewed everybody who said they loved me as a liar. My heart was broken yet again, but this time even more because now I put my trust in the Lord. I expected Him to protect me from all hurt, harm, or danger. When I was in the streets I had to expect the worst, anything bad was bound to happen. I never thought or imagined that evil things would happen to me now that I gave my life to Christ. I broke down all the way down. I couldn't get out of bed, I couldn't stop crying, I couldn't stop asking God, "Why?" I made up in my mind that I rather be dead than to deal with this.

The Breakdown

Oddly, suicide was always my way of dealing with my issues, so I contemplated it once again. There was a time when I stood in front of the medicine cabinet attempting to take every pill in there, but something wouldn't allow me to. Since I couldn't take the pills I decided to jump off the 105 freeway and end my misery, I couldn't do that either. So I begged God to take me in my sleep. I was at a point where I believed that death was better than my life I just couldn't win. I was tired of pretending like everything was okay. I was tired of smiling through my tears. I was tired of people humiliating me about my past. I was tired of being tired.

I refused to get out of bed or even leave my house. I just wanted to lay there and rot. Pastor Jarvis decided to come over unannounced to make sure I was okay and I wasn't. We talked for a while; well truth is he listened while I complained. Then he said something to me that quickly changed my attitude. He said, "If God delivered you before what makes you think that He can't do it now? The Lord did not allow you to go through all of those things and bring you here just to give up on you now."

From Porn to the Pulpit

When he said that something clicked and my pain suddenly turned into conviction. I began to cry out to the Lord, apologizing for doubting Him. After everything I've been through I should know the power of God. He delivered me from death how dare I think that He couldn't deliver me from this breakdown. I just needed to understand that attacks do come when you are in the body of Christ, but the Lord will never leave you nor forsake you. (Proverbs 34:19 Many are the afflictions of the righteous, but the Lord delivers him out of them all.) The devil does not like you, he wants to kill, steal, and destroy your relationship with Christ. (John 10:10) Instead of me crying and complaining about the obstacles, I should have praised the Lord through it.

I made a decision that day. I decided that no matter what may come my way, I was going to serve the Lord with everything in me. I wiped the tears away and I stopped feeling sorry for myself. I prayed for God to increase my strength, so that I could hold on to Him with a tighter grip when the enemy comes after me. I stopped caring about what people said or thought about me. I was sold out for Jesus and I was ready for a new beginning.

Chapter 14

A New Beginning

The tears stopped and my sorrows turned into joy. The words of my enemies didn't discourage me anymore. My haters became my motivators. The thoughts and opinions of people didn't matter to me. When my family, "friends," and some Pastors talked about me and didn't believe I was truly saved I didn't let it bother me. My only concern was proving myself to God alone. I knew that persecution was something I would have to face, but I wasn't going to allow it to stop me. (John 15:20 If they persecuted Me, they will also persecute you.) I was so focused on living for God that I didn't have time to pay attention to what other people were saying. What helped even more was when the Lord said, "If I tell you something believe it!" That meant no matter what people say or think trust God even when it doesn't make sense. As long as I did what He told me to do I was just fine. I was so determined to please Him.

I had my strength back. I started reading my Bible again, I prayed more; I got back to my Father's business! No more men, no more drama, no more self hatred. God showed me how to love Him first then myself. He gave me a new outlook on life. He showed me how to forgive and love those who misused me. He gave me a new relationship with my family. He gave me a new attitude. My lifestyle began to change abruptly. I'd only been back from New York a little over a year and already God was raising me up. I knew I was totally delivered and set free because I didn't have the same want for those old things. I didn't have the desire to do what I used to do, I didn't want to go where I used to go. I wanted to do what I was created to do which was praise and worship my God.

A New Beginning

My mindset completely changed. I wasn't angry, bitter, and unhappy. I had a "So What" attitude. So what if I did porn, so what if I was addicted to drugs. So what! It was over now. I was able to hold my head up in confidence knowing that I have been redeemed by the Lord. (Psalm 107:2 Let the redeemed of the Lord say so,)

Once again He reassured me that there is a true plan and purpose for my life, that's why I couldn't die. The enemy couldn't take me out even when I wanted him to. God didn't save me just to save me, I was made for ministry, I was born for this, and I didn't ignore it any longer.
(Jeremiah 1:5 Before I formed you in the womb I knew you; Before you were born I sanctified you; I ordained you a prophet to the nations.)

I accepted that I was called to ministry, but where would I start? What was I supposed to do? I prayed about it for a while and a few days later I was driving down Figueroa (a well known street where prostitutes "work") and I saw the girls out there and I started to weep. My spirit was so hurt to see these women out there selling themselves. I didn't want them to go through what I went through. In that very moment God said, "These are the women you're going to minister to, along with those who have been molested and abused; those who are bound in the same sin you were bound in. I'm giving you a deliverance ministry. I saved you so you can save others." After that I knew exactly what I was supposed to do. I've always been a person of action, a "go getter." I was ready despite what people felt or said about it. God gave it to me, now I was ready to get to work.

In January, 2010 I went to a church in Los Angeles called "Passion For Christ Movement." Pastor Justin Cox called people up to share their testimony. This was my opportunity to share what the Lord has done for me and as scared as I was I went up anyway. After sharing my testimony I saw how many people were touched by it. They had been through some of the same things I been through. There were a lot of people who were struggling with sexual immorality and molestation. When I saw their reaction I knew that God had appointed me for such a time as this. My life has never been the same since that night.

Shortly after that I attended S.O.V Ministry Training School in Norwalk. I was licensed and ordained in June. God has given me a powerful

A New Beginning

ministry. He sent me to schools, to jails, to the streets, and to churches to share my testimony and to let people know what God can do. My joy comes from doing Kingdom work. I now understand why I went through the things I went through. It wasn't just for me but it was for other people, it was for this ministry. God had a plan from the beginning. He knew exactly what He was doing with me. I devoted and dedicated my life to Christ. I went where He told me to go and I said what He told me to say. I was like Isaiah, here am I, send me! (Isaiah 6:8) My loyalty was to Christ not anything else. I allowed Him to give me a new beginning which included Him and Him alone.

He gave me a new joy, a new outlook on life and ministry. He gave me a new relationship with Him, a new love for myself. I was no longer ashamed or embarrassed. I loved the new person I had become through Christ and I wanted to share that with the world.

God gave me A New You Ministries. He put it on my heart to write this book. He put people in my life who have truly been a blessing to me. I travel all over the world sharing my testimony and preaching the Gospel. He allows me to mentor young girls to stop them from going down the same path as I did. He has opened so many doors of opportunity for me to give Him all the Glory and He's not done yet!

I understand that becoming a Minister, a Mentor, an Author, and founder of an organization is a blessing. It's a wonderful thing for Jesus to love me so much that He would show me favor to this extent despite my background. But the best part of it all is that I've become a woman of God. I've become a woman who has peace, a woman who has dignity and respect for myself; a woman who has mercy, love, forgiveness, and compassion for others; a praying woman. I've become an advocate for Christ. Most of all I've become a woman, not a "hoe" or the "B" word, but a woman.

I'm a new creature in Christ, old things have truly passed away. (2nd Cor 5:17) My past is my past. I've been forgiven and my sins are in the sea of forgetfulness. God has changed my name. Queen B the porn star is dead and Minister Danielle Williams lives. I'm not who I used to be. Those demons are gone! I have become a new person and I love who I am. It gets even better because you can do the same thing too!

Chapter 15

There Is Hope!

A lot of people reading this book have been through similar things or can relate to some of them. Maybe you've been molested, raped, or violated by someone. Or you've prostituted yourself or been addicted to drugs or alcohol. Maybe you've been ashamed of something that you've done. If that's you I want you to know that there is hope!

First of all, I want you to understand that there is no sin too big or too bad for Christ. Nothing you have done can separate you from Him. Trust me, I know this. I asked that same question for a long time; how can He love me after everything I've done? The answer is He never stops loving us no matter how bad we get. If you've fallen, but you're ready to come back home let nothing or no one stop you from seeking God. Ignore the haters, ignore your family, and so called friends get to Jesus! He's waiting for you.

Acknowledge that you do have an issue and ask the Lord to help you with it. Remember, we have not because we ask not. Do not be afraid to ask God to destroy an addiction or stronghold. Remove yourself from negative environments or anything that's going to tempt you to go backwards. Stay in constant prayer and trust in your heart that God is able to deliver you from whatever you're battling with.

If you're a woman and you've prostituted or stripped before and you're wondering how can I get my self-respect back, how can I move on when everybody remembers me from what I used to do? Don't allow people to hold your past over your head. If you know that you have genuinely changed their opinions mean nothing. You don't have to prove yourself to anybody. Ask God to deliver you from people and keep praising Him for your deliverance. Thank Him for setting you free

There Is Hope!

from that lifestyle. What you have is a testimony, don't be ashamed of it. Embrace it and share it. Hold your head up high. Forgive yourself and move forward. Remember there is no condemnation to those who are in Christ Jesus. (Roman 8:1) Don't worry about what people have to say just pray that they get delivered too. You are a new woman and your past is your past.

Those of you, who are suffering from a rape or molestation, suffer no more. Being violated can be the worst thing a person can ever encounter, especially as a child. I have gone through numerous attacks and I was able to get my healing from realizing that I am not a victim, I am a victor because I was able to survive it. The same goes for you. Don't you dare allow that person(s) to have control over you any longer. Forgive them, pray for them, and release them. Allow God to heal you.

If you are reading this book and you struggle with pornography or masturbation, there is hope for you. Prayer is definitely important, but you have a part to play as well. Remember faith without works is dead. (James 2:17) The first thing you need to do is get rid of every pornographic DVD you have and erase all the downloaded porn that's on the computer. Stay in constant prayer and believe God for your deliverance. It's not an easy thing to do, but it's definitely possible. You don't have to be embarrassed or ashamed about this everyone struggles with something. Know that God can and will bring you through this.

If you're bound by homosexuality and you're ready to break loose, there is hope for you! Whoever said homosexuals can't be delivered is a liar and the truth is not in them. Yes, homosexuality is a stronghold, but like lying it's a spirit that can be cast out. There is nothing too hard for God. You were not born that way, so don't believe that lie. Believe that God is, God will, and God can do all things. You have to pray and submit your mind and body to the power of the Holy Spirit.

If you are struggling with drugs, sex, alcohol, anger, etc. and you're ready to overcome their pull. The first thing you need to do is tell the devil it's over! Get on your face and cry out to the Lord. Kick, scream, yell, do whatever you need to do. Tell Him you're ready for a change because God won't move unless you are willing. Then go to whomever you trust (that's saved) and tell him/her you want help. It's not easy, but it's worth it. Change is worth

There Is Hope!

it, God is worth it! You can do it; it's never too late to change your life. Please don't be ashamed because all have sinned and fallen short. (Ro- mans 3:23)

Forgive yourself and do not beat yourself up for those past failures. Stay focused on where you want to be instead of where you were. There is hope, there is a brighter day, let no one tell you anything different. You are somebody in Christ! You are a chosen generation, you are a royal priesthood, you are a holy nation, and you are special!
(1Peter 2:9) Remember that you are the head and not the tail, you are above and not beneath.
(Deuteronomy 28:13) You can be whatever you want to be it does not matter how raggedy your past is. God loves you and he forgives all.

Turn your pain into power, your test into a testimony, and your trial into triumph! I believe you can do it, I know you can do it. The devil has no authority and no power over your life. I decree and declare you will be set free in Jesus name. (John 8:36) May God bless you always and forever.

The Danielle Williams Story…

I want to thank all of you readers, not only because you purchased this book, but because I want to thank you for trusting what God has done in my life and what He can do in yours as well. I pray that my story will be a blessing to you. Feel free to write me at expornstar3@yahoo.com I look forward to hearing from you. God bless you all.

Pornography Statistics

The pornography industry is a multibillion dollar industry. It has larger revenues than the top companies combined, such as: Microsoft, Google, Amazon, eBay, Yahoo, Apple, Netflix, and Earthlink; $13.3 billion in the United States, and $97 billion worldwide.

As of December 2005, child pornography has become a $3 billion annual industry.

Video sales and rentals accounted for $3.62 billion in revenue, while internet porn raked in $2.84 billion. Magazines were the least popular.

Pornography Time Statistics

Every 39 minutes: a new pornographic video is being created in the United States
Every second: $3,075.64 is being spent on pornography.
Every second 28,258 Internet users are viewing pornography.
Every second 372 Internet users are typing adult search terms into search engines.

*Top Adult Search Engine Request

Internet consumers are most likely to search for the terms "sex," "adult dating," and "adult dvd" to access their porn product of choice. The top 20 search terms also include "teen sex," and "sex ads." Men performed 97 percent of the searches for the term "free porn."

*Internet Pornography Statistics

The amount of pornography on the internet can be difficult to fathom. A total of 4.2 million websites contain pornography. That is 12 percent of the total number of websites. There are over 100,000 websites that offer pornography and 1 in 7 youths report being solicited for sex on the internet.

*Children and Porn

Access to pornography is available from early on. The average age of a child's first exposure to pornography is 11. A total of 90 percent of children ages 8-16 have viewed pornography online. 15-17 year olds have had multiple hardcore exposures. The largest viewer category for hardcore porn is teenage boys between the ages of 12-17. Pornographers use many character names that appeal to children such as "Pokemon."

When a child or adolescent is directly exposed to pornography it leaves lasting negative or traumatic emotional responses. They are introduced to sex before they are ready through images they do not understand.

*Adults and Porn

Pornography consumers access pornography both at work and at home. A total of 40 million U.S. adults regularly visit pornography websites. 10 percent of adults admit to an internet sexual addiction and 20 percent of men say they access pornography at work.

*Men and Porn

20 percent of men admit to accessing pornography at work. More than 70 percent of men from 18 to 34 visit a pornographic site in a typical month. 72 percent of porn viewers are men.

*Women and Porn

According to statistics, men are not the only ones to access pornography at work. A total of 13 percent of women admit to accessing pornography at work. One in three visitors to pornographic websites are women. 28 percent those admitting to sexual addiction are women. 70 percent of women keep their cyber activities secret. 17 percent of women struggle with pornography addiction.

1 of 3 visitors to adult websites, are women. 9.4 million women access adult websites each month. 13 percent of women admit to accessing pornography at work. Women, far more than men, are likely to act out their behaviors in real life, such as having multiple partners, casual sex or affairs.

*Christians and Porn

51% of pastors say cyber porn is a possible temptation. 47 percent of Christian men say pornography is a major problem in the home. 37 percent say it is a current struggle. 20 percent of church-going female participants struggle with looking at pornography on an ongoing basis. 50 percent of all Christian men and 20 percent of all Christian women are addicted to pornography.

Over half of evangelical pastors admit to viewing pornography last year. Roger Charman of Focus on the Family's Pastoral Ministries reports that approximately 20 percent of the calls received on their Pastoral Care Line are for help with issues such as pornography and compulsive sexual behavior. 33 percent of clergy admitted to having visited a sexually explicit Website.

Of those who had visited a porn site, 53 percent had visited such sites "a few times" in the past year, and 18 percent visit sexually explicit sites between a couple of times a month and more than once a week. 29 percent of born again adults in the U.S. feel it is morally acceptable to view movies with explicit sexual behavior. 57 percent of pastors say that addiction to pornography is the most sexually damaging issue to their congregation.

*The Negative Effects Pornography Leaves

Internet pornography is the new crack cocaine, leading to addiction, misogyny, pedophilia, boob jobs and erectile dysfunction. The internet is a perfect drug delivery system because you are anonymous, aroused, and have role models for these behaviors. The internet pumps pornography into your house 24/7, free, and children know how to use it better than grown-ups know how to use it. It's a perfect delivery system if we want to have a whole generation of young addicts who will never have the drug out of their mind. It causes masturbation, which causes release of the naturally occurring opioids. It does what heroin can't do, in effect.

Rabbi Shmuley says, "Pornography is incredibly harmful and destructive to marriages. Pornography subtlety undermines male respect for women by detaching a woman's personality from her body, reducing her to a mere sexual commodity. This in turn bores men and leads to dissatisfaction with their own wives and an inability to create a fulfilling, authentic sex life based on mutual respect for their female counterparts. Porn portrays all women in one of four degrading, dehumanizing categories. They're either a "greedy gold-digger," "mindless playmate," "insatiable nymphomaniac" or "one who craves pain." It gives you the most insidious view of women.

This can lead to an inability to form meaningful romantic relationships and even violence against women. Porn makes men get bored with their own wives. Excessive exposure to the incredible variety of naked bodies that you see in porn makes men feel permanently dissatisfied with their wives bodies.

Brie Hoffman says, pornography is bad for men because it causes men to have unrealistic views of a woman's body, to be unsatisfied with real women and to separate sex from intimacy which results in a life of loneliness, separation, lack of intimacy and impotence. Magazines use the most beautiful women to sell their wares and even those women are touched up and airbrushed. Pornography teaches men to look to the physical side of a woman rather than encouraging him to love her for her soul and mind first. The physical will change but the soul and mind usually stays the same.

Moreover, pornography teaches men to separate sex from intimacy and love. It divorces the sex act from relationship, which makes having a relationship difficult. In addition, it discourages the integration of love and intimacy which leads to a life of loneliness, separation and selfishness.

Some studies support the contention that the viewing of pornographic material may increase rates of sexual crimes. Some say a substantial exposure to sexually violent materials bears a causal relationship to antisocial acts of sexual violence. Violent people may watch violent pornography and are more likely to rape. Repeated exposure to violent and nonviolent pornography causes a likelihood of raping ratings and laboratory aggression against women. There is no longer any doubt that pornography inspires crime. Most child molesters admit that they consume hard-core porn on a regular basis.

Joe Beam says, porn is damaging to a marriage because most spouses feel as though it is cheating. It also takes the sexual energy away from the partner and towards the internet. The internet creates a fantasy that cannot be fulfilled by the partner so the addicted partner can only get their sexual needs met via the internet. Therefore sex does not happen in the marriage. Porn creates a set of expectations about sex in marriage that are quite literally impossible to fulfill. Because real people in real marriages eventually do not compare physically to those in pornography, porn usage erodes the ability to be sexually attracted to one's spouse.

Exposure to the multiplied variations of sexual behavior modeled in porn, they expect their partner to have sex in every manner possible, even ungodly acts. They also eventually compare themselves or their spouses to the people in porn. The person in a picture or video will never age a day or gain a pound, no matter how often the film is played.

However, spouses age, gain weight, and wrinkle. If a couple pursues porn, they will drift emotionally from their partners into an imaginary world that will never exist in reality. They eventually will reach the point where their lovemaking relies on fantasy and not at all on intimacy between them.

I could go on and on with the studies of pornography, but at the end of the day, we all know that it is wrong and damaging to us all. I encourage you to get help if you struggle with pornography. Help break this chain of destruction.

God Bless you.

Made in the USA
Lexington, KY
13 July 2016